"One of the finest books I have ever read. . . . impeccably written, taking a huge topic and making it accessible. . . . like a good friend talking with you over tea and a warm fire."

Krysta Kavenaugh, Editor-in-Chief
Marriage Magazine

"This is an unforgettable, deeply touching and honestly written book and I highly recommend it. It's not about fearing death—it's about embracing life."

Armchair Interviews
www.armchairinterviews.com

"An invaluable book for lay people facing a serious illness and death, it is also an important resource for health professionals. . . raw, poignant, funny, and provocative but above all, inspirational and instructional."

Mary Jo Kreitzer, Ph.D., RN, FAAN
Explore: The Journal of Science and Healing

"A wealth of knowledge, strength and comfort."

Kirkus Discoveries

"A heart-touching journey and uplifting inspirational resource for anyone going through life-or-death trials."

Midwest Book Review

"I have never seen anything like this book! Diane's perceptions are wonderfully original and illuminating."

Margaret Cruikshank, Ph.D., University of Maine
Author, *Fierce with Reality: An Anthology of Literature on Aging*

"*Living Consciously, Dying Gracefully* was. . . a joy to read."

James S. Gordon, M.D., Founder and Director
Center for Mind-Body Medicine, Washington D.C.
Author, *Manifesto for a New Medicine*

"Should be in every oncology clinic and chemo waiting room!"

Patricia Anderson, R.N., M.S., C.N.S.
Outpatient Psychiatry, New Ulm (MN) Medical Center

A Journey with Cancer and Beyond

By Nancy Manahan and Becky Bohan
Foreword by Bill Manahan, M.D.

Beaver's Pond Press, Inc.
Edina, Minnesota

ISBN 10: 1-59298-179-8
ISBN 13: 978-1-59298-179-3

Library of Congress Control Number: 2007920790
Printed in the United States of America
Second Printing: October 2007
11 10 09 08 07 6 5 4 3 2

Cover design by Robin Lewis
Text design by Clay Schotzko
Author photo by Diane Mock

Beaver's Pond Press, Inc.

Beaver's Pond Press, Inc.
7104 Ohms Lane
Edina, MN 55439-2129
(952) 829-8818
www.BeaversPondPress.com

To order, visit www.BookHouseFulfillment.com or call 1-800-901-3480.
Reseller discounts available.

Diane in Nursing School, St. Olaf College, 1959

When I was diagnosed with cancer in 1995, I knew that I was going to be open about that whole journey . . . Through being authentic, honest, non-perfect, and living the dichotomy—the yin-yang—of life in an out-loud way, I may have created a window into some people's own looking glass of their lives. Perhaps I have given them tacit permission to be vulnerable, to deal with life's gifts and life's uncertainties as they have been thrust upon me.

Diane Manahan
April 20, 2001

Contents

Diane finishing the Twin Cities Marathon, 1982

Foreword

by Bill Manahan, M.D.

In my thirty-five years as a family physician, I occasionally spoke with the spouse or child of a patient who had died recently. Sometimes my patient would describe the death as a "good death" or a "sacred experience." I was not sure what they meant by those words, but I was impressed that they seemed relaxed and at peace with their loved one's death.

Then it happened to me. My wife died of metastatic breast cancer. As Diane and I made the journey through thirty months of the spread of her cancer to other organs and the knowledge that her days were to be measured in months rather than years, Diane taught me more about living consciously and dying gracefully than I had learned in all my years as a physician. She showed me what a good death looks like, and what a sacred experience it can be for everyone involved.

I also learned firsthand that how we handle death is undergoing a cultural transformation as great as the one involving birth.

For most of recorded history, birth was considered a natural event that occurred at home with family members around the bed or waiting nearby. In the last century, however, birthing became a medical procedure that took place in hospitals, with the regular use of medical interventions such as spinal anesthesia, monitors, and medications. The family was usually excluded.

Lately we have witnessed a radical shift: many mothers are embracing a natural birthing process, fathers are often present during the delivery, and midwives are more accepted as an important part of the birth team. After the birth, babies are kept with the mothers, and breast-feeding is encouraged. Monitors are optional.

Likewise, for most of history, death was considered a natural event that occurred at home with family members around the bed. As technology developed, dying gradually became a medical event with invasive interventions used in an attempt to delay or prevent the inevitable. It became a contest in which death meant losing a battle. People tended to die in hospitals or nursing homes, often without the family being present.

We are now experiencing a deep cultural shift in how we view death. It is part of a natural process rather than a defeat or a taboo topic. More people who are near death are requesting to die at home rather than in the hospital. Family members and loved ones want to be present at the death. The hospice movement has educated the public and professionals alike, helping us to understand that it is not only possible but may be preferable to die in the comfort of our own homes.

My sister, Nancy Manahan, and her life partner, Becky Bohan, have written an accurate and heartfelt account of my wife's process that embodies the cultural shift toward death. From interviews and correspondence with friends and family members, from the journals Diane kept, and from their own experience with Diane, they have woven a thoughtful, educational, and beautiful book. It embodies the lessons Diane was here to teach and honors her memory as the conscious and graceful woman she truly was born to be.

I thank my wife for giving me the greatest gift that any human can receive from another human being—unconditional love and acceptance. Diane was, and still is, my greatest teacher, my favorite partner in play, and my best friend.

Bill Manahan, M.D.
Assistant Professor, Department of Family Medicine and Community Health, University of Minnesota Medical School
Past President, American Holistic Medical Association
Co-Founder and Director, Wellness Center of Minnesota

February 2007

Introduction

At her core, Diane Manahan was a healer and an educator. After spending seven years as a clinical nurse and eighteen as a psychiatric nurse, Diane started a new career at the age of fifty-one: teaching at Minnesota State University, Mankato. For ten years she taught young women and men how to be caring, competent, and compassionate nurses. It was no surprise that when Diane was diagnosed with breast cancer at age fifty-five, she approached her illness as a learning experience.

Although Diane lived a full and adventurous life, this book focuses on the years after her diagnosis because Diane's unusual approach to her cancer, her terminal condition, and her death is inspirational as well as instructive. She talked openly about her experiences and even shared them in her classroom. Although challenging at times, the subjects were not unpleasant to her. They were a natural part of her life's tapestry.

Her forthright approach contrasted starkly with so much in our culture that is afraid of death. Even most schools of medicine and nursing still pay scant attention to the dying process, giving only a few hours of instruction to their students, as opposed to whole courses for the other miracle of transition—birth. But avoiding the subject of death distances us from loved ones who may need support, and it cuts us off from part of our own spiritual journey.

A shift is occurring, however. The work of Elisabeth Kübler-

Ross and others on death and dying, the hospice movement, the introduction of mind and spirit perspectives into medical and nursing school curricula, and the increasing number of people who want to die at home are encouraging signs that we are opening to this change. In fact, many people are searching for new models for dying. This book shows one model of dying in a healthy, natural family and community setting.

Although Diane grieved deeply the loss of her health and of her life, she did not fear death, nor did she see it as an enemy. She only regretted leaving life so young. When her breast cancer was first diagnosed, she chose surgery, radiation, and chemotherapy, as well as complementary therapies. When it metastasized to other areas three-and-a-half years later, she and her husband Bill made a conscious decision not to pursue every treatment that Western medicine had to offer. She wanted the energy and emotional presence to spend the remainder of her time doing what she loved: teaching, playing, traveling, and being with her family and friends. She chose quality of life over quantity by refusing an all-out battle that would have left her weak, sick, and miserable during her last years.

As her death neared, Diane did not want to spend her last days in a hospital attached to tubes and machines, barely lucid. She told her sister, Patt, "I want to go on living until I die," and she did just that.[1] She was active until her last few days. Her holistic approach to illness, the richness of her life, and her spiritual strength may have helped her live so long and so well. When she died, her death was one of grace and consciousness, and one that honored the cycles of nature.

Indeed, Diane's deep connection with nature fueled her spiritual life and end-of-life decisions. She was raised Lutheran, attended a Lutheran college, and converted to Catholicism when she married Bill. Years later, she and Bill left Christianity when it no longer worked for them. Given her cross-cultural interests, she approached

---

[1] See "Appendix H: The Family Tree" and "Appendix I: List of People Mentioned and Their Relation to Diane" for information about people mentioned in this book.

religion as an anthropologist might. She learned about the religions of the countries where she lived,[2] explored why people held their particular beliefs, read a broad range of spiritual books, and attended conferences on spirituality. Diane adopted cultural anthropologist Angeles Arrien's four life principles synthesized from indigenous peoples around the world: show up, pay attention, tell the truth, and let go of the results.[3] She gradually developed her own spiritual life grounded in ethical choices, community service, cross-cultural spirit traditions, intimate relationships, and most of all, nature.

~

The two of us were with Diane when she died. It was the most profound and sacred experience of our lives. In the months after her death, we heard about the impact that her dying process had had on other people. After reading Dr. Janice Amatuzio's inspiring book, *Forever Ours: Real Stories of Immortality and Living from a Forensic Pathologist,* we realized that Diane's end-of-life story was just as extraordinary and moving.

We also realized that Diane's story should be recorded before people's memories faded. It had been four years since her death, and some of the details were blurring. So we e-mailed her family members and close friends, explaining our idea for a book.

We wrote about our own experiences of her death and interviewed Bill and many others who were involved. When we finished a draft, we solicited feedback. With each revision, the scope of the book expanded. Bill's offer of Diane's papers, including the typed journal entries and e-mails she had printed out and filed with other documents from her cancer journey, added immense power and depth to the book. We realized that the lessons found in Diane's journey and the stories surrounding her death were ones that might interest, educate, and inspire a much wider audience than the circle

---

[2] See "Appendix G: Timeline of Diane Jansen Manahan" for a list of places where Diane lived.

[3] Angeles Arrien, *The Fourfold Way: Walking the Paths of the Warrior, Teacher, Healer, and Visionary* (Harper Collins, 1993, pp. 7–8).

of friends and family that we had first envisioned.

The book has three parts. Part One recounts Diane's cancer journey, often in her own words. It records her thoughts, emotions, and decisions as she and Bill dealt with her diagnosis, treatment, remission, recurrence, and final months of life.

Part Two describes the day of Diane's death and the days immediately following as we experienced the end of her physical journey, the care of her body, and the celebrations of a life that had so deeply touched so many.

In Part Three we again hear Diane's voice in stories from people who have experienced some sort of communication or healing encounter with Diane after her death. These stories are a testament to the continuing presence and power of her spirit.

At the end of the book, a section called "Guidebook: Lessons from Diane on Dealing with a Serious Illness or Death" summarizes the lessons found in Diane's journey. It provides suggestions for dealing with the experiences that Diane and her family faced. It is meant to provide practical information and to encourage discussion. The lessons may not apply to everyone—after all, each person's path is different and each death unique.

The Appendices contain supplemental data about healing modalities, advice about getting one's affairs in order, and additional personal information about Diane.

We have several hopes for this book. First, that those who loved Diane will find solace in reading about her. Second, that the book can be useful to anyone who intends to be more conscious and grace-filled when experiencing illness or facing death. Third, that nurses, hospice workers, doctors, social workers, chaplains, patients and families dealing with end-of-life experiences might find Diane's holistic approach to dying helpful and informative. Fourth, that readers might be inspired and comforted by indications that the death of the physical body is not the end of our existence. Fifth, that people wanting to live intentionally and follow their values will feel empowered by Diane's story. Finally, we hope that the book is a tribute to Diane Jansen Manahan, one of the most fully alive people we have ever known.

Nancy Manahan and Becky Bohan
Minneapolis, Minnesota
February 2007

Bill and Diane Manahan, August 2000

The warp and woof of my life's tapestry has been my relationship
with my husband of 36 years, Bill Manahan.
That tapestry was strengthened and made even more colorful
by the privilege of raising and really knowing four sons.

As in the making of Persian rugs, where there is a flaw or a mistake,
there is no going back. It is simply there to be woven into the design,
to become part of the beauty of the masterpiece.
I am grateful for the opportunities to learn, whether through trials or
through joys.

My life tapestry is complete.
Grace exists in every thread.

Diane Manahan
Spring, 2001
[Three months before her death]

— PART ONE —

"This Long Journey with Cancer as My Companion"

Diane loved her life. It was a lush tapestry with rich colors and interesting designs. She was a graceful blend of wife, mother, friend, educator, holistic nurse, therapist, social activist, traveler, athlete, environmentalist, feminist, scholar, shopper, and musician.

In 1995, Diane and Bill's marriage was enjoying a renaissance. With their four sons establishing lives of their own, the couple was alone again, as they had been thirty years earlier. They enjoyed a comfortable intimacy, meaningful work, nurturing play, and precious time with friends and family. Life was good.

That year, as her August birthday approached, Diane recorded a list of objectives that illustrated her core values:

> As I begin my 56th year of blessed life on this planet, I have some goals in mind for the next few years, subject to

> change and definitely without attachment to their outcomes!
>
> To honor and be loving to Bill and our family and extended families
>
> To give back to my profession and community
>
> To be a friend the way one would want a friend
>
> To honor our planet and its creatures
>
> To trust in things or beings greater than I
>
> To call upon guidance from ancestors, known and unknown
>
> To work on being more generous and gracious
>
> To live as consciously as I can
>
> To retain a sense of humor about all things and to have the sense to know when not to laugh or speak up
>
> To be a little outrageous or slip up each day, remembering that I and others are so human

Little did she realize how these goals would resonate in the coming years. Five months after she wrote them, Diane was diagnosed with breast cancer.

Diane lived five and a half years on the "long journey with cancer as my companion," as she wrote in her journal. She believed cancer was a mysterious and sometimes scary presence, but not her enemy. Diane insisted that she was living with it, not dying from it.

It was a different design in her life's tapestry, but part of the entire work. She continued weaving until it was complete.

The chapters in Part One describe her journey—the diagnosis and treatments of the first occurrence as well as the metastases to other organs three years later. Diane's own words describe each step of her cancer experience, using healing philosophies that engaged mind, body, and spirit.

While her holistic approach engaged many facets of healing, it also acknowledged her own mortality. Diane fully lived every day she was granted, but she eventually turned her energies to planning her last days and saying good-bye to the many whose lives touched hers. She shared her journey openly and honestly, modeling a way to die consciously and gracefully.

— CHAPTER ONE —

The Journey Begins: Diagnosis

In December 1995, Diane felt a lump in her left breast. She had a biopsy five days before Christmas. It was cancer.

Given her good health, it seemed incredible. She and Bill had spent a week canoeing and camping in northern Minnesota's Boundary Waters that autumn. At age fifty-five, she was fit and full of life. How could she have cancer? How could her immune system have become so compromised? Although her mother had died of non-smoker's lung cancer at sixty-six, no one in her family had had breast cancer. Diane didn't have a genetic predisposition for it.

Diagnosis

Diane's first reaction to the news was disbelief. In her December 20 journal entry she wrote:

> CANCER. I am unprepared for this diagnosis. I don't believe that I, healthy, happy, Diane could possibly be harboring the big C . . . the report says that I have intraductal and infiltrating breast cancer. That means some of the cancer cells have left their ductal homes and are dancing around in the rest of my left breast. The tumor is 3 x 1.5 centimeters, a bit bigger than the knowing types like to see. But no lymph nodes can be clinically felt and last year's mammogram was negative.
>
> I am home only minutes and my dear dear friends who have been praying all afternoon call and ask to stop by. Laura [Turk] and Bev [Palmquist] do not know what they will find when they arrive. They think, like I did, that the pathology report will come tomorrow. They walk in with cheerfulness; I meet them at the door and say without fanfare or introduction: I HAVE BREAST CANCER. Their expressions will be imprinted on my heart forever. They dissolved into tears and hugged, hugged, hugged me. The three of us stood in the kitchen and wailed. They embraced wonderful Bill and we just stood there, stunned.
>
> Bill—my trusted love partner of many years. He has been steady, tender, close to me, instrumental in arranging all the many appointments that have to be done. I love him beyond anything I could ever write about.

Five days later, on December 25, Diane woke at 3:15 a.m. feeling anxious and restless. At 5:00 she wrote in her journal:

> I want so to keep a healthy spirit and attitude. I know there is no need at all to panic or fantasize about what might be, but I can't seem to stop my heart's pounding.

As she wrote about her fear, Diane felt calmer. She reflected on what was nurturing and satisfying in her life, especially having two of her sons and a daughter-in-law visiting:

> What a pleasure to have Topher, Tim and Kate here. They bring light just by their beings. There is much laughter, tenderness, attentiveness to everyone. What wonderful fortune to have them in our lives and in mine all the time but especially right now. Bill continues to be a model of balance: closeness yet appropriate distance, attentive but not hovering, funny, working but time for other things, loving while maintaining his life position or worldview that illness isn't bad and that this phase of our lives together means some extra maneuvering and possibly even some suffering in various ways, but it is not a tragedy . . .
>
> . . . And now it is Christmas morning. I just filled the stockings with care. I love Christmas. I just love so many things—the fresh air, walks, all the people in my life, twinkle lights, gorging on Christmas goodies, coffee, coffee ice cream, hearing Tim get so excited about food, the Messiah, my car!, my cello!, my computer! :), my clothes/shoes/jewelry. My god, how materialistic does one get. Well, so there it is—all part of me.

Three days later, after the children had returned to their homes, Diane wrote:

> Today I am having my first day to myself . . . It feels good to do a few things around here. I keep thinking I will spend time being philosophical or emoting. Nothing comes, so I will not force it. I think I am good with myself and the universe/god so perhaps I don't need to spend time being deep about it . . . As my wonderfully wise and caring friend Sue Towey says, it is part of the Mystery.

But the next day, December 29, a friend died of cancer. In addition, Diane's chest x-ray that morning looked suspicious. Diane wrote:

> Today was my worst day yet . . . Jan Barnett died during the night, and I had to return for repeat x-rays. This truly terrified me. Especially with Mother's lung cancer. I

> thought I would be starting out this whole journey with metastatic cancer.

The second x-rays revealed calcification of the rib, not cancer of the lung, a huge relief. Afterwards, Diane drove to the Barnett's home to be with Jan's husband and their children.

> They are courageous souls, not just to bear losing their mother and wife, but the remarkable way they are dealing with it. John is concerned about me! Maybe it helps ease his pain to think about others with cancer and what may be ahead.

Gathering Information

Now that the lump had been diagnosed, Diane needed to decide what to do. She didn't have immediate surgery as so many women with a breast cancer diagnosis are encouraged to do. She wanted to know her options.

But a hitch quickly developed. Although her primary physician had been open to her having a second opinion, when Diane requested a referral to a surgeon in the Twin Cities, she was denied because her managed care clinic and insurance would not allow it. She wrote to her clinic:

> Believe me, this adds to the stress and frustration of this whole situation! Choices definitely help people with having some modicum of control when we haven't been able to control our diagnosis . . . It feels like another blow. I am not alone, I know. But I feel alone when stranded by a system that doesn't consider all aspects of medical and health care.

Bill and Diane decided to go outside their primary care clinic for her surgery, even though it meant more out-of-pocket expense.

Their search for information continued. As a pioneer in the field of holistic medicine and a practicing integrative care physician, Bill had many contacts throughout the country. He called medical colleagues in alternative cancer centers; he and Diane talked to physicians, surgeons, and oncologists, getting recommendations about what to do and the best person to do it. They read articles, and searched the Internet. The more information they collected, the more it seemed that a mastectomy was unnecessary. Although removing the breast had been the norm, recent research had revealed that excising the lump resulted in the same survival rate. Diane finally decided to have just the lump, rather than her whole breast, removed.

The Lumpectomy

Diane's surgery took place two weeks after the diagnosis, on January 3, 1996, at Methodist Hospital in Minneapolis. The procedure went well and completely removed the lump. However, one lymph node out of twenty-two biopsied was positive. Cancer cells had left the breast and traveled into her lymph system.

> No! I wanted to scream. You don't have that right! There is a mistake. So close, yet soooooo far.
>
> This is tough for Bill and me. Another huge challenge and many more decisions about treatment: chemo or not, what else, nonconventional treatments, getting sick, losing hair, radiation plus chemo? I will just mutate into a radioactive turnip. Bill and I held each other. He was quiet; I cried . . . I want to live because I love my life. Do I love it too much? Naw.
>
> We walked outside for a little—the sun was actually shining. I always feel better outside. I think I will choose to die outside. See that little morbid thought just slid into this account. How to keep a positive attitude. So far, every time someone has said to me, Now there is an 80% chance you won't have this—I don't want people to say

> that to me any more even when they mean to be positive because it feels like a doom predictor. I called Bev and Laura, who came over. We cried and then cleaned the house! Cleaning is one of the great medicines.
>
> I totally ran out of energy by 7. One of life's small blessings these days is that Bill and I are both able to sleep at night. Right next to each other, just where we should and want to be.

The Pathology Report

Five days later, on January 8, the pathology report arrived. The news was not good. Diane didn't have hormone-receptive cancer cells, so a common treatment (Tamoxifen) was not available to her. In addition, her tumor was anaploid, a more aggressive type of cancer.

> I cried most of the day. I can't seem to control that. Funny—little crier Di all of a sudden. Bev and Laura were here patting me and crying and just being present. [School of Nursing Dean] Mary Huntley came by and we worked out the quarter class schedule. I'll teach my research class. I don't want to do all this. It sucks. Tomorrow is another day (this has a whole new meaning).

The next day, January 9, Diane felt better.

> Mother would have been 85 today. I am peppier. I love my resiliency; it is a blessing. The sun shines. The sky is blue. The downy woodpeckers are going at the suet.

On January 10 she had a scan to rule out metastases to the bones.

> Bev took me over for the injection of the radioactive tracer and we went out to breakfast afterwards. I sat in

> Baker's Square and looked outside at Red Lobster, as we were eating French toast, talking so casually about cancer. Bizarre.
>
> I went back for the scan at 11 with Pat Anderson [Bill's sister]. I had to have more pictures taken and that really scared me. It turned out all right. I was so relieved that I started to cry in the radiologist's office. I came home and walked in the beautiful snow.

Two days later, Diane wrote:

> My spirits are better. I do have a formidable decision to make. I can't quite decide whether to have chemo or not. It feels like violence to my body. I respect my body, yet I want to remove traces of little cancer colonies if they are present. I really am stumped. I will be talking to some people soon and reading to help with my decision . . . I talked to Bob [Christensen, Bill's cousin, a surgeon], who said if I am going to do chemo I should do it as primary treatment and not wait and have it later. It then becomes palliative rather than curative. I talked to Chris Northrup [a medical colleague and friend of Bill's], who said sometimes self-sufficient women need to hand over their care to someone else and be fed (as in breast-fed!) by someone else. Having chemo is one way to do that. She also suggested a medical intuitive reading . . . and taking Chinese herbs and possible acupuncture during the treatments.

Now that the type of cancer was known, Diane was stepping into that labyrinth of decision-making that accompanies most people with a serious illness. What medical options were available? What were their pluses and minuses? What complementary options were available? What were their pluses and minuses?

Diane and Bill, both immersed in medicine for their entire careers, were about to enter a new terrain: the world of cancer treatment.

— CHAPTER TWO —

The Journey Continues: Treatment

What next? Neither Bill nor Diane was a cancer expert. Bill, whose background was in family medicine, had just joined the faculty of the Center for Spirituality and Healing at the University of Minnesota Medical School. Diane, who was a clinical nurse in her early career, had for decades been practicing psychotherapy and then teaching college. Neither was familiar with all the terminology, procedures, medications, and research studies for breast cancer treatment. Although they had much to learn, they knew they could work as a team to weave a care plan that drew in the threads from many areas of healing.

The Chemotherapy Decision

The conventional medical care plan for breast cancer involves three steps: surgical removal of the cancerous tissue, radiation, and chemotherapy. The first step had been completed—the tumor had been removed. Since at least one lymph node was affected, it made sense to begin radiation, which would rid the surrounding tissue and lymph glands of lingering cancer cells.

The more difficult decision was whether or not to have chemotherapy. Diane didn't like the idea of putting large doses of chemicals into her body, and Bill had serious doubts about the efficacy of chemo for her type of breast cancer. Throughout his medical career, he had felt comfortable challenging conventional treatments of diseases, including cancer. He already had learned that with Diane's stage and type of cancer, chemotherapy resulted in a seventy-five percent survival rate after five years. Without chemotherapy, the survival rate was around sixty-five percent. Were those odds worth going through the rigors of chemo? Most people would accept chemotherapy on the chance that they would be in the lucky ten percent.

In addition, the medical and social pressure to take the conventional route was enormous. Diane's doctors and her friends wanted her to do everything possible. If Diane rejected chemotherapy, how much support would she receive? If the cancer returned, would she feel at fault for not doing everything possible to prevent it? Should she take the chemo to prevent possible disapproval and guilt?

In his medical practice, Bill sought clarity, consistency, and understanding as he partnered with his patients in their care. He now used the same approach with his wife as they carefully weighed the choices of treatment. Ultimately, Bill knew, the decision was Diane's.

After much discussion and reflection, Diane decided to follow her oncologist's recommendations of chemotherapy. Although it wasn't what Bill would have done, his support was immediate and unwavering. "I loved her no matter what decisions she made," Bill explained. "We'd had differences on many other things. For example, I preferred to live simply, while Diane enjoyed doing more and having more than I did. But we were partners no matter what."

On Tuesday, January 23, 1996, Diane began radiation treatment five days a week for thirty-three sessions. Believing that a positive attitude was crucial to healing, Diane tried to maintain an upbeat view. During her radiation treatments, she would call up images of favorite places or "beam" herself to loved ones, visualizing their affection and support.

The next week, on January 31, she began six months of CMF chemotherapy (Cytoxin, Methotrexate, and 5-Flurouricil), receiving an intravenous dose on the first and eighth days of the month and taking a chemo pill for fourteen days.

She was surprised at how weepy she was after the first treatment. She didn't dwell on the sadness, however. She imagined, instead, that the tears were washing out her body like a great cleansing stream of water.

A Path of Peace

Diane had been a student of nonviolence for many years. She had read Gandhi, Martin Luther King, Jr., and other spiritual-political teachers. She and Bill served with the Peace Corps in Asia and Africa. During the Vietnam War, she was involved in nonviolent anti-war activism and had participated in the Mother's Day March on Washington in 1971. Suddenly, three decades later, she found herself immersed in the battle language of cancer treatments.

> People would say to me: "We're going to kill those bastards. We're going to fight this." It was like a war mentality. And a lot of the cancer literature also reveals a war mentality. That approach may work for some people. It might give them the motivation and the impetus they need to be an active part of their own care. But for me, that didn't fit. I wanted to know how I could be active and proactive in this process without being at war.
>
> Being nonviolent about the cancer did not mean that it was okay to have it or to compromise with it—saying you can have that organ if I can have this organ. I definitely wanted the cells out of there. They were uninvited guests. But I needed to acknowledge the cancer cells—that they were doing what they were programmed to do. And I needed to find ways to invite them to exit and hurry up about it.

Diane redefined chemotherapy to be more congruent with her philosophy of nonviolence. Rather than imagining toxic chemicals killing the cancer cells, she welcomed the infusion as a source of nurturance and healing: "I saw it as a river carrying the cancer cells out of my body," she said. Sometimes she envisioned the chemo cocktail as "milk and honey. A little Merlot. A touch of nicotine. A splash of Häagen-Dazs coffee ice cream. A twist of navel orange."

Another step she took was to regard each chemotherapy appointment as an opportunity to nurture relationships. Early on, her friends told her she didn't ever have to go to her appointments alone. Diane took them up on their offer and throughout her months of treatment, invited a different friend or family member to each chemo session, wanting to share the experience with as many people as possible. Each person had an hour of uninterrupted time with Diane, sitting in the cancer center while a needle dripped "milk and honey" into her vein.

Complementary Therapies

Once the decisions regarding standard medical treatment had been made, Diane and Bill turned their attention to complementary care. Both of them had been active in the holistic medicine movement for many years before Diane's diagnosis, she as a member of the American Holistic Nursing Association and the creator of her university's first course in holistic nursing, he as a founder of the Wellness Center of Minnesota, a founding member of the American Board of Holistic Medicine, past president of the American Holistic Medical Association, and the author of a book on dietary causes of common medical problems.[4] Together they researched complementary approaches that could promote healing from cancer.

The options were overwhelming. Allopathic medicine had three treatments to offer: surgery, radiation, and chemotherapy. Comple-

[4] *Eat for Health: Fast and Simple Ways of Eliminating Diseases Without Medical Assistance* (H J Kramer, Inc., 1988).

mentary medicine presented hundreds of options. Diane felt overwhelmed with choices. At the same time, there wasn't enough information about how each complementary therapy worked with radiation and chemo. At times she grew tired searching for reliable information that simply did not exist.

Nevertheless, she and Bill read widely and talked to colleagues. Gradually, they developed a care plan that included several complementary healing modalities.[5] Their tactic proved to be effective: Diane had very little fatigue during her six weeks of radiation therapy. Even during chemotherapy, to the amazement of her oncologist, whom Diane kept apprised of every approach she was using, she didn't suffer from the normal chemo fatigue, rarely experienced nausea, and never lost her hair. Diane's care plan included seven nutritional elements.

Shark Liver Oil. The first step Diane and Bill took was to find shark liver oil, which is believed to boost the immune system and suppress cancer. From consulting with experts in alternative treatments of cancer, they found that this oil could also be an excellent energy-support during radiation therapy. Diane took one capsule in the morning and evening.

Cabbage Juice. Every morning during the six months of chemotherapy, Bill juiced carrots and green cabbage and blended half a cup of each juice to make a drink that is believed to counteract breast cancer. (Red cabbage works too, but Diane didn't like it as well and it didn't yield as much juice as green cabbage.) Later Bill wondered how much of the healing power was in the juice itself, and how much was in his preparing and serving it to his wife every morning and afterwards cleaning the messy juicer clogged with the remains of the vegetables.

---

[5] See "Appendix B: Complementary Treatments Used by Diane" for a full listing of Diane's complementary care plan and descriptions of each component.

Soy. Studies show that eating soy may be helpful for breast cancer and other hormone-related tumors such as prostate and uterine cancer. Diane increased her intake of soy products, mostly in the form of tofu and tempeh (cooked fermented soybeans that can be used in place of meat). She also used soy milk on cereal.

Low-fat, High-fiber Diet. Although many people radically change their diet upon a cancer diagnosis, Diane chose not to do so. A big change, such as a macrobiotic diet, felt stressful to her, and she did not want to add stress to her life. Her diet was already fairly low-fat and high-fiber, so she ate the way she usually did. However, she did allow herself just a bit more chocolate and Häagen-Dazs ice cream.

Supplements and Antioxidants. Each day Diane took a multivitamin and mineral tablet with carotenoids that gave her the recommended daily requirements of nutrients. Since the oncologist cautioned against taking high levels of antioxidants during radiation therapy, Bill and Diane waited until three weeks after the radiation treatments stopped before increasing her intake of supplemental antioxidants, which are believed to slow or prevent cancer by protecting cells from damage caused by free radicals.

Fruits and Vegetables. Diane increased the amount of fruits and vegetables in her daily diet, and after the radiation, she included extra cruciferous vegetables, such as cabbage, broccoli, and cauliflower, which are abundant in antioxidants. Diane loved green salads, so eating more of them was a pleasure for her.

Intravenous Vitamin and Mineral Cocktail. Twice a week during chemotherapy, Bill administered an intravenous infusion of vitamins and minerals called the Myers Cocktail to reduce side effects and strengthen Diane's immune system. With the full knowledge of her doctor, Bill prepared the mixture at home and sat with Diane for the hour it took for the solution to drip into her vein.

While physicians are generally encouraged not to participate actively in the care of a family member, Bill did not hesitate to do so. He had treated Diane and the children during their Peace Corps years in Malaysia and Africa and later while practicing in rural Minnesota. Rather than going to even more medical appointments, Diane appreciated having her IV in the comfort of their home, and it felt natural for Bill to administer the vitamin and mineral infusion.

~

These, then, were the nutritional ways that Diane complemented her traditional medical treatment. She said later that botanicals, or natural plant-based medicines, such as essiac tea, probably would have played a greater role if she had known about them earlier.

Diane also used many other complementary healing modalities. For example, she received regular Healing Touch, acupuncture, and massages, which balanced her energy, reduced stress, and supported her immune system. They also helped to relieve the lymphedema (swelling) in her left arm caused by the removal of lymph nodes when the breast tumor was excised. Diane did special exercises to reduce the swelling and maintain the mobility of her arm. She also practiced Qi-gong exercises, prayed, meditated during outdoor walks, and consulted with medical intuitives.[6]

Healing Energy

While Diane and Bill juggled medical appointments, decisions, and emotions, and even found time to make presentations about their cancer journey at professional conferences and workshops, they had constant support from family and friends. People visited, called,

[6] See "Appendix B: Complementary Treatments Used by Diane" for a full listing of Diane's care plan and descriptions of each component. "Appendix A: A Summary of Healing Philosophies" provides an overview of different approaches to health care.

prayed, and sent cards and letters. Diane was deeply touched:

> It is truly awesome. I am brought to my knees by some of the messages, the love, the anguish that a few people write about. I had no idea about their feelings about me. I also know that they write and speak of themselves, especially women, for they become very scared about breast cancer. There is so much hype about it. Then healthy Diane goes and gets it . . . Ms Health Prototype or something—and causes a real scare among women for themselves and men for their partners. I hope all the men are a little nicer and more tender for all this.
>
> I want to do something creative with some of the messages, both on the cards and of people's thoughts. I don't know what or how yet. I also kind of like being on so many prayer chains or in individuals' prayer life. What can I get from all of this positive stuff? Let them baby me, says Sister Ramona, who I saw today. "Just let people baby you, Diane. It's okay. Actually it is wonderful," she said. Take it in, take it in. Well, if positive vibes, negative ions, love waves, prayerful intentions, and healing amulets can do their thing, I have it made!

Diane sometimes had what she called "healing moments," encounters of special energy and love that felt like times of healing, whether of the body or the spirit. She wrote of an episode early in her radiation:

> This morning's healing moment was so big that it classifies as a . . . heart orgasm . . . I have . . . two men friends who are at radiation each morning the same time I am. John and LeRoy have become pals and we have lots of fun joking around, especially about all the friends and relatives I bring with me to treatment. They tell me that either I have many friends who care about me, or I can't keep a friend very long. Or the friends can only stand coming with me one time. Then they laugh.

> When Laura and I arrived this morning, John and LeRoy were already there. An older man who has treatments before me was still there with his wife. As a surprise for me, Bev was there having coffee with the gang. So Laura walked right up to Bev and gave her a hug. John said, "I wonder if she is giving those away?" That catapulted Laura into action. John stood up for his hug, then LeRoy, then the older couple, and then each of us hugged each other until it made about six hugs per person. As I hugged the elderly man . . . I said "I think this is healing for us cancer patients, don't you?" He looked at me with slightly watery eyes and said in rural southern Minnesota fashion, "You bet." We were all whooping and laughing when the radiation technician came out and wondered what was going on. Fun happens here, says the lovely nurse Barb. Good things.

As part of her emotional support, Diane carried with her a small white drawstring bag. Inside were over a dozen little objects that friends and family members had given her to represent their healing intentions or that she had selected for their special meaning. These "amulets," as she called them, included a jade dolphin that her son Tim had brought from New Zealand, a small, smooth stone inscribed with "Dream," and dried flowers from her walking trip with Laura in Scotland. During chemo treatments, Diane would take out all of the charms and explain to whoever was with her that day what each object meant to her. It was a way to deepen relationships and to focus on the loving energy that was supporting her.

One treasured gift not in her bag was from her oldest son:

> Michael knew I was sprouting canker sores in my mouth . . . Later that evening he arrived with a little purchase—a tube of numbing stuff for cankers. So thoughtful. So loving. So tender. He's so quiet about his caring and it hits deep within me.

Life Continues

Diane kept up her busy work and social life during chemotherapy. She wanted to keep her life as normal as possible, yet enhance it by doing things that gave her pleasure. Soon after the diagnosis, she withdrew $20,000 from her 401K retirement account and had $800 transferred into her checking account each month. It was "free money" that she could spend to visit family and friends, buy plane tickets for her children, see alternative healers, and make purchases she would normally think too extravagant, such as a beautiful gold ring she spotted in a jeweler's window.

On a warm summer evening after her chemo treatments had ended, she gathered her intimate female friends and family members in the woods of Seven Mile Creek Park north of Mankato for a special ceremony. The women spoke from their hearts, performed rituals of healing, sang, ate, and celebrated that Diane's chemotherapy was over.

Diane still seemed fit and healthy. Everyone hoped her breast cancer was gone for good.

Diane at Lake Superior, 1995

— CHAPTER THREE —

Remission

After her radiation and chemo treatments in 1996, Diane's life resumed its normal flow. Between December 1996 and March 1999, Diane taught a seventy-five percent load at the university, earned a Master's Degree in Nursing, served on three boards, traveled, and actively nurtured relationships with her friends and growing family. By now she and Bill had three grandchildren: Tessa and Teliz, the children of David and Jill, in California, and Jansen, the son of Tim and Kate, in Michigan. She loved to visit them, her other children, and friends.

The Cancer Support Group

When Diane was treated for cancer, she discovered that there were no support groups in the Mankato area for cancer patients. In 1997, she worked with the Open Door Health Center, a clinic serving poor and underinsured families in Southern Minnesota, to organize a women's cancer group, which she facilitated until six months before she died.[7]

Eleven women joined the group, and Diane found they needed no prodding to talk. Everyone was willing to share her story. Usually the talk centered on medical issues such as the group members' reactions to their cancer treatments. Diane noticed that the other women weren't as interested as she was in discussing spirituality or emotions like fear, sadness, rage, frustrations, or disappointments. Letting them take the lead, she didn't push them into uncomfortable territory. Everyone in the group was already experiencing enough discomfort as it was. The group could be safe and accepting.

Over time, the members became close and called each other often. If someone was absent from a meeting, everyone noticed.

During the last six months of her life, Diane gradually transitioned out of the role of facilitator, and one of the original members took over the task. That group, with changing membership, is still meeting, and it remains Mankato's only cancer support group for women. It is called "Diane's Hope," in honor of its founder.

Cancer's Shadow

During these years of remission, Diane would feel that loneliness common to many cancer survivors. She missed the support she had received from her extraordinary health care team. Outside of the cancer support group, almost no one mentioned her experience. It was as if her cancer had never happened.

Were the people who had prayed for her and sent caring cards and letters still keeping her in their prayers? How could she say anything about this strange feeling without sounding selfish and morbid? Her cancer experience had become the elephant in the room that no one acknowledged. What do people do in this situation? She had no answer.

[7] In a report to the clinic, Diane recorded her observations and lessons learned from facilitating the cancer group. They are summarized in the Guidebook at the end of this book.

In the back of her consciousness was the awareness that cancer had been present and the knowledge that it could return. She wrote in her journal in late December 1998:

> Three years since diagnosis. Every year brings a better prognosis. Sometimes I find it hard to believe that the cancer ever happened at all. When I read about it or go to cancer group it becomes real again. Sometimes I find myself thinking about my funeral. I don't know what that means and I surely do not want to create my own reality. It just comes to me...then floats away.

Diane had regular checkups. For three years the news was good each time. In January 1999, she rejoined the community chorale, which stages an Easter performance of Handel's "Messiah" every year. After a few weeks, she developed a hoarse voice. She thought it was from the colds and viruses going around as well as all the singing she was doing. As it turned out, she was wrong.

— CHAPTER FOUR —

Metastasis

In March of 1999, Diane and Bill attended a holistic cardiovascular conference in Hawaii. Diane hoped her hoarse voice would get better with the relaxation and the warm moist air. However, it seemed to worsen. At one presentation, Papa Henry, a well-known native Hawaiian healer, looked at her for a moment and said, "I need to see you alone."

After the workshop, Diane and Bill met with him privately, and he shared his intuitive "reading" of her body's energy:

> Papa Henry told me that my cancer had spread to my chest and throat area and that my heart was bad. This was alarming, but Bill and I felt he was talking energetically. He gave me some herbs and said things would be okay if I took them and prayed and didn't worry.

Later Diane wondered if "things would be okay" meant that she would be cured. Or that if she died, it would be all right.

Inoperable

When Diane returned from Hawaii, her doctor scheduled a CAT scan. It revealed a small (1.5 centimeter) mass lodged around the carotid artery under the breast bone. The left vocal cord was paralyzed because of the tumor's pressure on the upper chest nerve that supplied the vocal cord. This was the cause of her hoarse voice.

A biopsy would be difficult because the mass was under the breast bone and hard to reach. Since it was lodged against the aorta, any surgery would risk a lethal nick to the main artery. Also, Diane's doctors suspected there were most likely other sites of cancer.

Diane responded to this news in her journal:

> It is now the wee early hours of April 18. I am strangely calm and shaky all at the same time. In a weird way, the knowledge that I don't have to do anything for this is relieving. The other side of that, of course, is that I will die within months. Or a few years, I hope. I just don't know now.
>
> I don't want to analyze this. I don't really care what I am to learn from this. I simply have it; didn't want it or ask for it. Now my task is to decide how I will go though this time. Perhaps it is a gift to know when you are going to die. Yesterday I put some clothes together to give away. I can get things in order. I can live each day truly like it might be my last. I can stop thinking about other things and concentrate on what has the most heart and meaning to me. There is an ephemeral quality to this—like I am talking about someone else, a surreal and depersonalized atmosphere. Bill and I can even laugh about it at times; and we cry too.

New Goals

Diane decided not to "forge ahead with a biopsy" but to wait to re-scan the area after she and Bill returned from a long-planned thirteen-day hiking trip along the Norwegian fjords to celebrate their thirty-fifth wedding anniversary. In addition to this, her primary goal was to be well enough to attend her son Topher's wedding in September. She wrote that it would be a year of "time with my beloved, time with my friends, and healing. Of believing in what I have chosen for a course now." She also hoped to celebrate both her and Bill's sixtieth birthdays in August and September of 2000, sixteen months in the future:

> How I get there is up to me and all the angels and universal energy and prayers and my family and friends. Please, help me with the grace to be natural and not forced, to be loving and forgiving, to have the energy to get this house where I feel comfortable in leaving it, to really live each day and not take too much time up in fretting, planning, pining and wishing, playing "if only." This cancer doesn't deserve that much power!

Continuing Therapies

Diane had a full summer and fall in 1999. She and Bill loved hiking in Norway. She felt in good health and hiked even on the day Bill accepted a ride to the next hut. She wanted to experience as many of the fjords and mountain trails as possible. She and Bill didn't know if they had a year or ten years together. They simply enjoyed the moment.

Laura accompanied Diane to Hawaii for three days to see Papa Henry again. He prescribed specific herbal infusions and reassured her that all would be well. She and Bill also took a number of short trips, including one to their son's wedding at Lake Tahoe, a peak experience for them both.

When school started that fall, Diane applied for tenure and promotion, still thinking positively. She continued with her mind/body/spirit therapies. In a November 1999 journal entry, she detailed her health regimen:

1. Try to live the Blessing Way (pray daily, give gratitude daily, do one life-affirming action daily).
2. Be with nurturing people as much as possible. Let go of toxins of all types.
3. Do two Qigong exercises a day—one for balancing and one for lymph drainage.
4. Do stretching exercises daily that Tim taught me. My neck area is very tight.
5. Do at least ten deep breaths a day.
6. Go to speech therapy weekly and try to remember what we work on for my voice and choking.
7. Take the two teas recommended by Papa Henry (Uhaloa and Ki-nehe).
8. Do exercises recommended by Jamie Champion. Continue to see him every three months.
9. See Qigong Master Chunyi Lin twice monthly.
10. Continue with internist (October's physical and mammogram were good).
11. Keep in touch with my oncologist.
12. Exercise and eat foods that are base rather than acid.
13. Vision a positive future. Delete negative thinking when I can.
14. Love.

Shifting Dynamics

As 1999 wound down, Diane felt lost at times. Always a people person, she found herself retreating more and more from people. It was unsettling. Her voice was weak and it had become tiring to talk. Her breathing was not as easy as it had been. The dynamics of her life were shifting.

In December, as she reflected on the past year and contemplated the coming year and new century, she had "many thoughts and wishes whirling":

> My biggest wish is for a peaceful land and place for our grandchildren. They are stepping into a century that is promising technically, genetically, and, hopefully, spiritually. I want to pave that way for them. My ways of doing that feel meager, yet okay and meaningful simultaneously: loving contacts, gifts of time and thoughtful items, teaching in a non-teachy way, being a loving grandparent, reading to them, being there whenever and however is possible.
>
> I feel good about how I live. I spend money in ways I want to, I love my life with Bill in all ways, I love our children and their families, I love our friends and their families. I like my job very much . . . It is always a privilege to assist students of nursing and life on their journeys. Could I do better in all these areas? Of course.
>
> And so I carry on, living each day with gratitude, an occasional pout, a big grin, and a heart and soul that soar with delight . . . as I snuggle up to my life love at night. I also am blessed with a great sister and family to love and be loved by. Hey, besides, I drive a Volvo, so . . . on to the waiting adventures of 2000!

More Cancer

On January 4, 2000, Diane had an MRI. The results were devastating. She sent a letter to her friends telling them the news:

> Each suspicious area turned out to be metastases of my cancer. I kept thinking, "Well, one of these will be good news." Not. The short of it is that I now have visible cancer spread to my left lower lung, right lobe of my liver and an enlarged chest tumor that puts some pressure on lymph and blood flow, though that is very manageable at this point . . .
>
> I rely on your loving energy, caring and prayers or sacred intentions. Thank you in advance. I am struggling with this new and unexpected turn. It is bleak; I know I will have some emotional resilience in a few days but it is too fresh right now. I see myself as a healthy person who happens to have cancer, so how can this be happening? I feel good except for shortness of breath on exertion. I still want to teach, though I will cut my load some in order to spend intentional healing time.
>
> I am blessed with wonderful physicians and a caring staff at our cancer center. My colleagues at school are also caring and willing to help. My family and friends here are beyond any expectation I would dream of.

The following week Diane started weekly intravenous injections of Herceptin, a new non-chemotherapeutic drug. It was hoped the drug could slow the rate of the cancer's growth, but at that point, nothing could stop it.

Although she was receiving Herceptin, Diane focused on natural healing and joy, rather than enmeshing herself entirely in the medical system. She received regular Healing Touch therapy as well as acupuncture and herbs from a traditional Chinese medicine practitioner. She consulted with other healers and spent time out of doors every day. She wrote poetry, journal entries, and letters. She did spiritual reading and visualizing. She played her cello. She wanted to be as healthy and active as possible so she could squeeze out every minute of life and enjoy the last months of her relationships.

Bill had been working three days a week at the University of Minnesota Medical School in Minneapolis and two days a week as the medical director of Open Door Health Clinic in Mankato. Now he cancelled two half-days of his work week so that he could go to appointments with Diane and be home with her more. Diane finished her January 4 e-mail with this description of her husband:

> Bill is steady, present in all ways, and loving. His peaceful countenance teaches me by example about joy and acceptance of the moment. So you can see how rich my life is. I just want to experience it for a long time!

— CHAPTER FIVE —

Playing on Three Strings

During the year following the spread of her cancer, Diane was still relatively healthy. Her voice was weakening, though, and when she exerted herself, she was more short of breath than before.

Just as her body was changing with the growing cancer, her spirit was undergoing transformations. She was adjusting to a shortened life and making the necessary physical and emotional accommodations.

A Different Approach

After the first diagnosis of breast cancer in December 1995, Diane had tried to understand why she had the disease. Was it genetic? Was it environmental? There are toxins in the air, soil, water, household cleaners, cosmetics, personal care products, and food. Was it personal? Was something wrong with her thoughts or her personality that had caused her to get cancer? Could her cancer have some relation to the collective unconscious? Many years before her diagnosis, a psychic had told Diane she carried in her fibrocystic breasts "the generational tears of women."

Now, three years later when Diane learned that the cancer had metastasized to the point of being inoperable, she took a different approach.

> . . . the first time I got cancer in 95–96, I wanted to be self-reflective, and I was kind of hell-bent to find out . . . what it was telling me so that I could be a better person or do what I should be doing . . . [Now] I have less interest in that. And I have some interest in not trying to figure things out at all, and just trying to "be" with it. Because where I think I was unsuccessful, at least in my own mind, was in finding some deep meaning . . . This time I don't have much interest in reflecting.

As a strong proponent, practitioner, and recipient of holistic healing, Diane was aware of a range of attitudes concerning illness. When she read or heard people say about their cancer, "I'm a better person for it" or "My cancer made it possible for me to learn about myself and change my ways," it didn't resonate for Diane. She didn't want to turn her disease into a moral lesson. Nor did she want to get into a "blame the victim" mentality:

> I think one of the injustices of the holistic or the wellness movement—and Bill and I have talked about this a jillion times—is the guilt that comes with being sick. Or if it's not guilt, it's that there's a reason. And there's a lot of literature about the "cancer personality." Well, I thought I would never have cancer because I'm really far from that personality profile [of holding in feelings, being angry or depressed, having unfinished business]. And so when I got cancer I was really embarrassed. I didn't want to tell anybody I had cancer because then they would look at me as a cancer personality.

Diane could laugh at her embarrassment, but it revealed her awareness of popular notions and her rebellion against them. As usual, she found her own path: just being with her cancer, the companion who had joined her on her journey once again. The reason didn't matter. It just was.

The days had a new slant to them. When starting a new page in her journal, she mused:

> How something as simple as starting a new page takes on a different meaning now. Each day is a new page. I used to barf at the saying "Today is the first day of the rest of your life." Each day a new beginning? I don't know, not really. I just ask for guidance at being an instrument of peace for me and others every time I have the privilege of waking up.

A Life Review

After the metastases, Diane had what she later considered a pivotal healing experience with her young friend, John Lofy. John asked Diane if she would like to talk about her life while he recorded the conversation. Diane was thrilled with the idea. John arrived from Michigan in April 2000, and for two days he interviewed Diane and Bill. Diane's voice was raspy from the metastases to her vocal cords, but hour after hour she talked until there was nothing more to say. John transcribed the tapes himself and presented Diane and Bill with a 128-page typed spiral-bound transcript.

Until now, Diane had focused on continuing to live fully. A few weeks earlier, a friend had said to her, "I don't know what to do. I've never been with someone who is dying."

"I'm not dying," Diane said curtly. "I am living with cancer."

According to Bill, within a week of the interview Diane had a perceptual shift. They were walking in Sibley Park one morning before going to work when she said, "Bill, after telling my story to John, something has changed. I feel like now that there's a record of who I am, maybe it's time to start thinking more about how I want to die and making plans for my memorial service."

"Diane!" Bill exclaimed, stopping short and turning to face his wife. "This is the first time you've talked about dying!"

Diane had turned a corner. She started planning for her death and envisioning her memorial service in detail. She now seemed able to look unflinchingly at what was waiting on the horizon.

A Grain of Sand, Indeed

Although preparing for death, Diane did not withdraw from life. Far from it. She continued her activities and enjoyed relatively good health. In the summer of 2000, she and Bill camped in her beloved Boundary Waters Canoe Area with Laura and Jim Turk, who planned a route requiring only one portage. Laura says that Diane seemed to find comfort in saying, "The rocks will still be here, the loons will still be here, the trees will still be here, the lakes will still be here." Understood by all were the unspoken words "even when I'm no longer here."[8]

In a July 2000 journal entry, Diane reflected on life and the perpetuity of nature:

> So, who do I think I am?? That I really matter on this planet?? That things on this earth will stop if I am seriously ill, or die?? What kind of bravado and arrogance have I been experiencing? When I observe even the people around me, nothing really changes because of my life-threatening condition. Did I expect or want that?? Some days I do. I am embarrassed by wishing that. By wishing that someone would: a) not go to work as usual and say I am going to think about Diane today or go see her; b) be sad all day; c) not feel happy for a time; d) by having my station in life really really affect them. Well then, let the embarrassment begin. Because some days I feel this way. Do I really want my family and friends to suffer in this way? To change their own lives because mine is changed in a major way from what I/we expected? The bottom

[8] See Diane's poem "Loon Calls" on page 47.

line is NO I don't. But a couple lines before the last one, maybe a little bit. At least today.

Things go on for me too. I live each day just about like I always do, though more consciously and intentionally. I see more; feel more (sometimes I don't want to do that); and appreciate more. I feel both more shy ***and*** more bold. Never know which it is going to be!

By experiencing the fact that I am just a grain of sand among trillions and just one wave upon the endless lake or ocean that recycles itself, I also know in spades that I am connected to everything and everyone. The larger the beach, the larger body of water is always there in various forms. Maybe my next realization will be a star in the sky. Think of how miniscule one celestial body is in that universe!

There are new adventures ahead, new frontiers I can't know about now. Grain of sand indeed.

Heartfelt Communication

As part of her preparation, Diane continued to share her journey with others. After a walk in Sibley Park in late January 2001, Diane e-mailed her friends:

The landscape around the park was sparkling clear today. The river had its usual places of open running water surrounded by ice and snow. There were four people flying down the sliding hill, screaming their guts out. It warmed me to see them so. My innerscape was not so clear.

After all these five years I am not any closer to understanding this mystery than on day one. I am more peaceful with not understanding it, and almost don't care what the rhyme or reason is . . . Let it go, I tell myself.

Anne Lamott said, "Grace meets us where we are but

> does not leave us where it found us."[9] Indeed, I am not where I was five years ago or one year ago. I am enriched, grateful, less physically strong, heartfully intact, and sometimes lost.
>
> I share my story because I love you and you love me. Healing isn't an event but a moving process or flow and I am riding the stream. This helps me float.

Later that month, after another walk in Sibley Park, Diane sent an e-mail to several people with more "musings":

> Does having a life-threatening condition or disease make one more "holy?" In one's own eyes, or in the eyes of others? Are holy and sacred the same? Do people think more of you if you have a life-threatening condition? Should they/we? I have always felt holiness in each and every one of us. Though I am more tuned in to this than ever, it seems that I feel less holy and more human-with-fault than before. Kind of curious, I think. Sometimes it tickles me that people (such as colleagues) say things to me that they never would otherwise, such as, you are such a sweet person, Diane. Sweet? I don't see myself as sweet, maybe a moment or two. Then I wonder if some holiness is evident that I don't see or know about.

John Lofy's sister, Annmarie Rubin, responded to Diane's e-mail from her home in Michigan:

> I think what makes [a terminal illness] holy is that we are so afraid of death . . . we avoid everything relating to it—we avoid thinking about it and talking about it and admitting that we will all have to do it . . . Now you have journeyed into the eye of cancer . . . You face death. You talk about death . . . You stand on the edge of life, Diane, and you look with eyes wide open at the vast landscape in front of you and behind you, above you and below.

[9] Anne Lamott, copyright © 1994, reprinted with the permission of the Wylie Agency, Inc.

> And then you tell us about it. You do it in such a way that makes us (or me anyway) almost breathless.

Diane loved Annmarie's letter. "You can't know how valued it is," she wrote to her friend.

> You generously said that I look with eyes wide open at my landscape of life. Yes, sometimes. And other times, I feel like my eyes are wide shut. Shut tight, with the glue of denial, stagnation, irresponsibility keeping them closed. As in falling asleep, sometimes I see dancing pictures on the insides of my eyelids. If the picture happens to fall on negative and fearsome fantasies, I open them! And then, there it is—today and how wonderful life is at this moment . . .
>
> I find your writing about facing death alone as a sacred experience fascinating. It is the ultimate silence as we can know it in this age and culture. Sometimes I want to be able to come back in some way to tell you all about the fantastic experience I will have. Then I realize that that would take away from each of your own experiences and how that will be sacred for you, too . . . I don't feel frightened of death itself. Curious and a bit excited, even. I feel very patient and willing to wait to see what that will be like.

Annmarie's father Chuck Lofy also responded to Diane's e-mail. Chuck and his wife Mary had been Bill and Diane's friends for thirty years, occasionally spending long weekends together on the lakes of Northern Minnesota. Chuck wrote:

> I do not have cancer but I am aging, and am becoming—as I approach seventy in July—increasingly and vividly aware of my mortality . . . Next to me as I write this is a picture I treasure of Annmarie, standing in the twilight on the water of a bay with Lucy, her dog, looking at a beautiful sunset. The photo tells me not just about Annie, but about all of us standing small and with our ani-

> mals and animal-selves, lost in wonder at this magnificent world we live in, brought to silence in the silence and power and beauty of nature . . .
>
> I see you in this way, as dancing in the face of the vast expanse of time and space and your own moment in it. You have affirmed life, and existence, long before your cancer, long before I met you. I see you living or shouting your existence out loud, in full color, laughing (as Gibran put it) all your laughter and weeping all your tears. That is how you are, as fully alive as anyone I have ever met . . .
>
> You have always been an embodiment of that ideal for me, balanced and human, playful and serious, naughty and holy . . . all at the same time. That balance is for me your dominant trait.

Diane felt, in her words, "deeply honored" by Chuck's response. She elaborated on what he had written:

> Einstein said once that what is . . . most important is beauty and harmony. I have tried to live in harmony with the part of me that is cancer-filled. Can we not just exist together? I ask my cells. Can we be harmonious and compromising in that I will give up some things dear to me (singing, breathing easily, playing tennis or hiking hard) if you stop your onslaught and just reside within this host called Diane?? There is room for us both. I think if we can come to this agreement, we will both live in harmony, even holiness. Is it possible for a destructive force such as a cancer cell to be holy? I think so.

Palliative Care

As the "destructive force" put pressure on more organs, alternative mind-body-spirit therapies continued to play an important part in providing palliative care—the relief of pain and discomfort. They included Healing Touch, Chinese herbs, acupuncture, Qigong, prayer, spending time with friends and family, and being outdoors in nature. Her grandchildren were a major source of joy. Diane now had a fourth—Owen—born to Tim and Kate. As she wrote to her friends:

> I feel blessed in many areas of my life, if not all . . . These blessings become vivid in color and richness as I take each day as a gift. Each of you is among that bounty that so enriches my life. I have such support in every arena, including my colleagues at work and an excellent health team. My spiritual life feels deep and rich, enhanced by reading, reflecting, recapitulating, sometimes ranting, sometimes raving. My four darling grandchildren both tickle my heart and stir tenderness beyond tears. They light the path ahead . . .

Diane loved teaching and wanted to stay in the classroom until the end, and she did, using a wireless microphone so her students could hear her. For the 2000–2001 academic year, she cut back her teaching load to sixty-seven percent, but taught both fall and spring semesters, sharing her cancer journey, when appropriate, with her colleagues and nursing students.

On March 20, 2001, Diane was, as usual, walking the half mile from home to her office at the university when a shooting pain in her left groin forced her to stop. She called Bill to pick her up. X-rays revealed that the cancer had spread to her hip, pelvic bone, and cervical spine.

She notified her nursing colleagues of this development:

> Dear Friends,
>
> So much can happen in a week's time. As you notice by now, I am "on the cane" again, only this time not because I am waiting for a hip replacement but because I have significant metastasis to my left hip and pelvis. After testing and many consultations, I am beginning palliative radiation as of today (March 29).

Unfortunately, it doesn't stop there. The bone scan also revealed metastasis to my cervical spine. We are all worried about that area. I have decided to go ahead and have my neck/throat radiated as well and will begin that next mid-week. So my already compromised voice will get another set-back, but that is preferable to other possible consequences. These are all hard decisions for me.

I have had a great fourteen months since learning of my extensive metastases and feel quite healthy in general. I trust my healthy parts will serve me well through this bout of treatments as well. I am truly fortunate to have continuing and wonderful support from you here at school, my husband and my family and friends, and a finely-honed health team, the members of which are working well together, including the "alternative" members. My spiritual life deepens, even on my dark days.

I surely can take a lesson from the famous violinist, Itzhak Perlman [who, because of childhood polio, uses leg braces and crutches]. The story is that he struggled to center stage for a big symphony performance and prepared for his solo. After a few bars of music one of his violin strings snapped. The audience moaned to think he would have to struggle off the stage, get another string and begin the arduous process again. But he surprised everyone by signaling the conductor to continue. He adjusted the music and his solo to playing with three strings instead of four. His music, though different from what was expected, was beautiful nonetheless. The audience loved his impromptu improvisation of his "work."[10]

And so I will learn and continue to teach, to be a friend, to live on two or three of my strings. Let the improvisation begin . . . . . .

Diane

[10] For more complete descriptions of the Itzhak Perlman story, see the websites www.wtv-zone.com/Mary/PLAYINGAVIOLIN.HTML or www.chodoshguitar.com/articles/Itzhak.html.

Loon Calls

Hear it? Hear it?
Now we know
Look quickly before she sounds
In the Boundary Waters we row.

Many calls mean many things
Like us, and how we talk.
Cooing and clucking
Over our flock.

Silence reigns in this place
We tend to fill it with our clutter
Chatter, pans, songs and chopping
Stop! An eagle's wing aflutter.

Loon turns into lune at night
Its sliver shining brightly
Stars agaze in complex groups
Bill holding me tightly.

Thankful for these two blessed days
Friends…comfort…ease
Everything is now a delight
Even simple crackers and cheese.

Rocks that beckon
Rocks that us do warm.
Water though chill is clear and deep
A clean campsite is our norm.

Chop wood; carry water
That's our mantra there
Dip, dip and swing our paddles
Will walleye be our fare?

Cards at night, storytime, too
Our tent is not our castle
Four adults asleep in there
Really without hassle.

Nothing feels tragic while in this loon-ar magic.

Diane Manahan
Summer 2000

Cancer Fatigue

Cancer, treatment, scans
Tests, medicine, appointments
Words that made a home
In my head.

Herbs, soothing touch
Prayers, talk, love
All made a home
In my heart.

Upbeat, grateful, smiling
Patient, active, normal.
Friends along my
Way.

Wonder, envy, longing
The uninvited guests
Have over-stayed
Their welcome.

Tired of smiling
Tired of appointments
Tired of living the moment
Tired.

No predicted end to treatment
There is no remission, no break
A cloud shadows my path
Cancer fatigue.

Diane Manahan
January 30, 2001
[After twenty-one months of metastases]

— CHAPTER SIX —

Orchestrating the Finale

Once Diane had made peace with her own death, she was ready to jump into action to prepare for it. She wanted to do so while she was still feeling relatively healthy rather than waiting until she no longer had the strength. From making a four-page list of personal items to be bequeathed to spending time with everyone she loved, Diane did a hundred things to prepare for death during her last months.

Creating a Remembrance for Her Grandchildren

One of Diane's few regrets was that she would not see her four grandchildren grow up. It troubled her deeply that they were too young to remember her clearly. She decided to make a scrapbook for each one. She wrote notes about herself and described the qualities she treasured in them. She selected pictures and poems for the grandchildren. These scrapbooks were a tender testament of her life and her love for them.

Planning Her Death

A book that profoundly influenced Diane was *Alison's Gift: The Story of a Thousand Hearts Opening,* a gift from her daughter-in-law, Kate. The book recounts the true story of seven-year-old Alison Sanders, fatally injured in a car accident. Her mother, Beth Sanders, stayed with her brain-dead daughter in the hospital, grieving, receiving visitors, and making arrangements for the care of Alison's body and her funeral. A friend played soothing music on her lyre for hours on end. When the life-support machines were turned off, Alison's body was brought home and placed on her own bed. Dry ice preserved her body during the three days of the vigil, a round-the-clock flow of family, friends, and Alison's schoolmates.

Later Beth founded Crossings: Caring for Our Own at Death, an organization dedicated to in-home after-death care.[11] Diane and Bill sent away for the Crossings kit, which provided step-by-step directions, a description of state laws governing the handling of a body, and special materials for keeping a loved one's body at home. They spent a lot of time talking about what Diane wanted. She wanted to die at home. But how exactly should her body be handled? Where should the visitation be—at home or at the mortuary? And which mortuary? What type of celebration could honor her life? What would happen at it? Who would participate? Where would it be?

By the end of June, Bill had written a four-page, single-spaced document that described what Diane wanted when she died. Given that no one knew exactly what would happen at the end, Diane agreed that the plans should be flexible. For example, she wanted to be in charge of her pain medication, but if the pain couldn't be controlled at home, she could be taken to a hospice facility.

Diane and Bill visited mortuaries until they found a mortician who welcomed their unusual ideas and gave them information to help them plan. Hank Kolbinger at Landkamer Johnson-Bowman Mortuary in Mankato said it was one of the few times a person with

[11] See "Recommended Resources" at the end of this book for information about Crossings.

a terminal illness had interviewed him. He agreed to work with Bill and Diane in whatever way they wished. Hank was impressed with the active role that Diane took in the preparations. He said that most people leave the arrangements to the family.

After Diane decided on cremation, she wanted something special to hold her remains. One night Bill called their youngest son and asked him to make a box. Topher, a builder and carpenter, researched the specifications (thirteen inches by seven inches by six inches deep). He found a piece of recycled redwood that had a natural flaw resembling a loon. It seemed perfect for Diane, who loved listening to the loons in northern Minnesota's wilderness areas.

Diane's friend, potter John Glick, also contributed. He made a small clay urn for each son and one for Diane's sister to hold some ashes. Most of the ashes would go into Topher's redwood box for Bill to keep.

Planning Her Life Celebration

In the months leading up to her death, Diane spent time visualizing and organizing her Life Celebration. By the very act of planning it, Diane was able to continue her heartfelt connections with those closest to her. As Bill explained, "She drove the operation. She brought people to the house and asked them to participate. She had a lot of fun doing it."

She parceled out tasks to dozens of people, who felt honored to be included. She asked certain friends and family members to speak and her sister-in-law Vanda to organize the refreshments. Vanda later commented that Diane "knew she was worthy of celebration, which sends a message that we all are—that we should claim a final tribute, and design a unique crescendo for ourselves."

When Diane asked her niece's husband, Jon Olseth, to sing a song, he was so overcome that he volunteered to write one! He played it for her on July 3, eleven days before she died, and she was very moved by it.[12] Jon learned how therapeutic writing a memorial song could be. Four months later, when his brother died in a mountain biking accident, Jon wrote a song for David as part of his grieving process.

The week before she died, Diane called a family meeting at her bed. For two hours she talked about her Life Celebration. She had already delegated many of the tasks. Still, things like the programs and decorations had to be done, as well as bookmarks that she wanted handed out to everyone.[13]

Loving nature as she did, Diane wanted her celebration to be outside. Sibley Park was an obvious choice. In a letter to her St. Olaf college friends, Diane explained that the park was:

> . . . where I have spent many hours walking and checking flowers, sledding with our children, checking the river, and last fall I organized a walk there for cancer and its relationship to the environment. I told Bill this morning as we discussed my Life Celebration that it sounded like something I'd like to attend!

Designating Memorials

Throughout her life, Diane had always been engaged in her community no matter where she was living. In Ghana she helped in the schools, in Malaysia she volunteered as a nurse, in Kenya she worked in public health, in Minnesota she served on boards of community service organizations and participated in support and social groups. One of her core principles was to give back to the world, and now she wanted her memorials to benefit the community.

Diane gave much thought to who would receive monetary gifts upon her death. In the end, her choices reflected her loves and were congruent with her values:

---

[12] See "Appendix F: 'Diane's Song' by Jon Olseth" for the lyrics.

[13] See page 109 for a copy of the poem on Diane's bookmark.

~ *Nature*: Mankato's Sibley Park, her favorite spot to walk, picnic, and be with friends and family.

~ *Community and fitness*: Mankato's YMCA, where she swam regularly and served on the Board of Directors.

~ *Support networks and environmental activism*: Minneapolis' Women's Cancer Resource Center, which provided counseling about treatment options and sponsored educational programs on the environmental causes of cancer. (The Women's Cancer Resource Center closed in 2006.)

~ *Nursing education*: A special room at the Minnesota State University, Mankato School of Nursing where students could have a quiet space to relax, reflect, and study, rather than having to dash across campus to the student union between classes.

The Horizon Shortens

On May 9, on a day Bill was teaching at the Medical School in Minneapolis, Diane went to her Mankato oncologist with her friends Laura and Bev. After her x-rays were developed, the three women walked into the consultation room and saw them hanging across the view boxes. White dots representing tumors lit up the film like a tangle of Christmas lights. The cancer was everywhere.

The doctor gently told Diane to go home and be with her family and friends and enjoy every single moment. All the treatment would end, he said, with pain medication being the only consideration at this point. The three friends were stunned. They wept. They drove immediately to Sibley Park to let the natural world embrace them while they tried to absorb the news.

Two days later, on the last day of spring semester, Diane woke up and looked in the mirror. Her eyes and skin looked yellowish. She walked to campus as usual, taught, met with students, and did paperwork. At 4:00 she returned home and joined Bill on the deck.

Bill looked up from his book. "Oh no, Diane!" he cried. In just a few hours, her skin and eyes had turned deep yellow.

They both knew what profound jaundice meant: complete liver failure. Just three weeks earlier, her liver functions had tested quite normal. They hadn't expected this disastrous development so soon.

Diane consulted with her Minneapolis oncologist, who said that in her experience, most people with liver failure live between two weeks and two months. There was nothing more the medical world could do for her. Diane prepared to turn in her final grades and clean out her university office.

The next day, Saturday, May 12, a group of Diane's close friends and family members gathered for a late afternoon picnic in Sibley Park. Diane wanted to be outdoors as much as possible, and she loved picnics. Her sister-in-law Pat Anderson and her mother-in-law Ruth Manahan drove twenty-five miles from Madelia to join her.

Ruth cherished Diane like a daughter. They both loved to travel, play bridge and tennis, shop for clothes, and entertain friends. Ruth indulged her daughter-in-law's love of little stashes and kept a bag of peanut M&Ms in a special drawer just for her.

Over the years, they had enjoyed a running joke about a laundry issue. Diane always refused to learn how to bleach stained linens. She saved up her soiled tablecloths and dishtowels for Ruth to bleach and iron. Ruth loved doing this chore for Diane, but would affectionately chide her, "I won't always be around to do your bleaching. You'll have to learn someday." Now that day would never arrive.

Ruth brought to the picnic the beautiful diamond ring she had wanted Diane to inherit. She asked Diane to wear it and enjoy it for as long as she could. She wept as she laid the golden circle in the palm of Diane's jaundiced hand.

After the picnic, the family drove to the home of Diane's brother-in-law, Jim Manahan, who was celebrating his newly-earned degree in Spanish. Although tired, Diane actively participated in the party. Her yellow skin signaled how little time she had left, but she didn't try to cover up. She wanted to continue doing what she normally would for as long as possible.

In fact, Diane craved "normal" activities. A month later, in early June, Laura Turk took her to the home of a friend who had a swimming pool. They floated on rafts all afternoon, basking in the sun. Laura says that Diane repeatedly said, "Oh Laura, this feels so 'normal.'" Another day, the two friends went to a favorite restaurant for that most typical of American lunches: a cheeseburger.

Nancy Manahan and Diane
Sibley Park, May 12, 2001
The day after Diane's liver shut down

— CHAPTER SEVEN —

The End Draws Near

As the end of June drew close, Diane continued with her activities, but her energy level was flagging. Her jaundice, which had started the second week of May, was now advanced, and she was losing weight rapidly. Her skin was quite dark and her eyes very yellow. She walked with deliberation. Knowing that Diane's time was running short, family and friends gathered to support her.

Living with Determination

A few weeks before her death, Diane got the urge to buy something red to wear and asked Laura to go shopping with her. She bought Laura a red top too, not only taking care of her own needs but turning it into a gift for a friend as well. Later, Diane wanted something nice to die in. Laura bought her the prettiest pair of pajamas she could find, a three-piece set made of soft white flannel sprinkled with red and pink roses, with pink piping around the edges.

Ten days before she died, Diane attended the Fourth of July parade in St. Peter, Minnesota. She sat in a wheelchair on the boulevard with friends and family members ranging from her toddler grandchildren to her 89-year-old mother-in-law. Afterwards, she attended a picnic at her nephew's home, another normal family experience.

Over the summer, Bill and Diane's home had filled with people. Tim and Kate and their two boys happened to have the summer free between the end of Tim's residency and the start of his medical practice as a doctor of osteopathy. David and Jill and their two children came from California. Topher and his wife also visited, and Mike, who lived in Mankato, dropped by often. Diane's sister Patt and her husband arrived from Arizona and stationed their fifth-wheeler in a nearby park.

At least fifty people brought stews, soups, casseroles, and salads during those weeks. Laura coordinated food deliveries among Diane's book group, colleagues, and friends. The family never had to cook a meal—they would just make a salad and heat up what had been dropped off.

In those last few weeks of her life, Diane often saw guests three times a day—in the morning, afternoon, and evening. They were friends from St. Olaf College, colleagues from the university, her book group, choir members, and others. Some friends flew in from New Jersey, Montana, and California to be with her for a few hours.

After a visit, Diane would collapse, sleeping deeply to gather her strength. Then she would sit up, straighten her hair, put on lipstick, and be ready for the next visitor. As her daughter-in-law Kate said, "She was determined to do her work."

Bill, meanwhile, had cut back his work schedule further so he could spend more time at home. He seemed calm, almost glowing with love, as he welcomed visitors, talked and played with his children and grandchildren, took care of routine household business, and tended to his wife. He and Diane made dying at home feel like the most natural, normal thing in the world. They both radiated a deep, quiet peace and joy that enveloped everyone who entered their home. It was obviously holy ground.

Itching

Kate helped bathe Diane, who found that water and oatmeal soap soothed her. She also loved being gently scrubbed with a loofah, which helped relieve the itching caused by the bile acids accumulating in her body after liver failure. Bill would sometimes take Diane into the shower stall and have her perch on a ledge while the water drummed on her.

Diane wrote about the persistent itching in her journal:

> Death by chocolate? Death by drinking? Death by cancer? NO...................
>
> My death may come from incessant itching and scratching. There is no controlling it, either the itch itself or attending to it by its demand of scratching. No wonder I am losing weight rapidly for I am in constant motion. It is consuming and takes away my ability to really concentrate.
>
> When people ask me how I am, they understand cancer fatigue, stomach distress or any pain. They do not understand how disconcerting constant itching is and how it just wears me down. After all, it isn't really painful or life-threatening.
>
> Hey, just slather on the Schlomberg's or calamine lotion. Ignore it. Take some Benadryl. Nope, I will just hire a scratcher to follow me around and scratch pretty constantly, moving site to site to keep me somewhat comfortable. Death will still be elusive.

Despite her physical discomfort, Diane could still make humor out of her situation. One day after Kate helped her out of the bath, Diane moved in front of an open window. Completely naked, yellow and scrawny, she looked across to the house next door and pretended to see her neighbor.

"Oh, hi Don!" she said with a coquettish smile and flutter of her hand.

Getting Weaker

Diane kept up a steady stream of communication by phone, e-mail, and letter, as well. On July 6, eight days before she died, Diane went outside to say goodnight to Bill and their grandson Jansen, who were "camping out" in a tent. Afterwards, she climbed the stairs to her bedroom for the last time. As she paused before attempting the last two difficult steps, Kate heard Diane coaching herself to "Just do it!" with the intensity of a marathon runner hitting the wall. However, she was too weak, so Kate and Tim helped her up the last steps and into the bedroom.

That night Kate wrote in her journal:

> She is functioning on reserves now. She rarely eats. Her pain has created a need for morphine which makes her nauseated. Then she is weak, dizzy and a bit disoriented. So then she goes off the morphine patch, eats and then when the pain re-emerges, back to the patch. Diane and Bill call this a "dance" not a "vicious cycle"—they're fundamentally at peace with what is going on.
>
> She is so grateful for everything. She still asks nicely for what she wants and musters the energy to say "not just yet" when something unneeded is offered.
>
> She talked about "what if..." today up in her office. Without Bill's ability to modify meds and having extra help around, she'd be hospitalized—and she said she'd probably be dead by now. What exists here is truly amazing.

In fact, twice during her last two weeks, Diane would have been rushed to the hospital if her husband and son hadn't been health practitioners who were familiar with seizures, at peace with the dying process, and not given to panic.[14] It also helped that Bill was coordinating pain medication with Diane's physician and that

---

[14] For someone dying at home without a family member who is a health practitioner, hospice offers similar support in case of a seizure or other emergency.

he had morphine in case she needed it.

One night, Diane began having severe pain in her liver area. Although she had the morphine patch prescribed by her physician, it could only deliver a low dosage over a long time. She woke up Bill and he immediately gave her an injection of morphine. They waited for it to take effect, but the pain increased. Diane was writhing on the bed and moaning. Bill gave her another shot of morphine. After a few minutes, the pain subsided, and within fifteen minutes, she was sleeping comfortably, in her own bed.

The second incident happened a few days later. Diane had convulsions, probably caused by the metastasis of the cancer to her brain. Although seizures are common, are not painful or dangerous, and end naturally after a few minutes, they can be terrifying to people who have never seen them before. Bill helped Diane lie on her side to keep her airway open, made sure she didn't hit her head on anything, and let the electrical storm in her brain play itself out.[15] Afterwards, he comforted her and told her what had happened. Like most people who have seizures, she didn't remember anything of it. Then he let her rest and prepare for the visitors that afternoon.

Drifting

Although Diane continued to see visitors, she was starting to lose her grounding in this world. On July 6 Kate wrote:

> I get the impression Di lives right now for socializing. She uses all her energy to prepare for and receive guests. Tim commented this evening that she seems to be separating from her body . . .
>
> Two times tonight she said how strange she felt. She's never felt like this before. She's unable to focus . . . She's feeling out of control and it feels a bit scary to her . . . Here again, it seems like a separation from body.

[15] See "Helping Someone During a Seizure" in the Guidebook.

One day as Diane drifted in and out of consciousness, she motioned Bill over to the bed. He put his ear close to her mouth to hear her. She whispered, "Bill, you promised you'd cremate me."

"We will, Diane, but you're not dead yet," Bill replied.

Diane said, "Oh."

She was fortunate to have so many family members and friends tending to her needs. They were able to relieve one another and provide support during these intense days. It was, however, emotionally draining for the caregivers. As Kate observed in her July 6 journal entry:

> I love Diane. I've felt weepy all day to see her so depleted. After she collapsed into the bed with my arm around her, she said, "This sucks." I am sorry she's uncomfortable. She is so amazing. Everyone thinks so, that's why people are steadily coming to pay their respects.

Upstairs, Diane received a stream of visitors. People would sit with her, talking, telling her stories, or if she was too tired to interact, sitting in silence. Often music played in the background. Throughout her illness, friends had sent her tapes and CDs with their favorite healing music. Now that music provided comfort.

Diane never became incontinent, nor did she ever lose her beautiful silver gray hair. She was able to eat normally until a few weeks before her death. She regulated her pain, but accepted or rejected every dose of morphine on her own terms, in her own time. She wanted to be alert when she had visitors. She wanted to be as fully conscious as possible throughout the whole experience.

Two days later, Kate wrote:

> She said in short whispers: "I can't breathe enough... so...I take...lots of short breaths. Every time...I breathe in...it hurts. Though...I took care of people...in this way...as a nurse...I had no idea...the pain.
>
> Kate...I feel...so fortunate...to have you...in my life... Listen...to the joy...Bill and Jansen...have." We heard

> laughter bubble up from the living room. "The tenderness," she wept. "My friends are awed by Bill's generosity." Just then Bill greeted Bev, who'd arrived for a visit. A combusted joy, "HI BEV!" Di said, "Who else...would greet...my friends...like that...for me?"

Getting Close

During the last three days of her life, someone was always with her. Bill usually stayed with her at night, waking when Diane would stop breathing for long moments, talking with her when she couldn't sleep.

Sometimes she would wake up and say, "Aren't I dead yet?"

"No, Diane," Bill would whisper back, "you're still here."

"Why can't I die, Bill?" she asked repeatedly. "I'm ready to go. Dying is harder than I thought it would be."

All he could do was gently hold his wife and comfort her through these poignant nighttime conversations as she tried to discover how to leave her body.

Kate wrote in her journal:

> She is getting close. Today I was alone with Di and said, "I feel like you are getting ready for a big journey and I have an urge to pack you a sandwich."
>
> "I wish you would!" she replied.

On July 13, 2001, the day before Diane died, Professor Mary Huntley, Interim Associate Dean of the School of Nursing, came to the house to tell her that the university administration had given approval that day for the special room for nursing students. It would be called "Diane's Room" in honor of the woman who had seen the need, envisioned the space, and helped make it a reality. Mary described Diane's reaction to this news:

> She raised herself up from the bed to hug me. I held her. By then she was very weak, so it was remarkable that she was able to do that. I helped her lie back down . . . we said goodbye and I sang:
>
> > Shalom to you now, shalom my friend.
> > May God's full mercies bless you, my friend.
> > In all your living and through your loving,
> > Christ be your shalom, Christ be your shalom.[16]
>
> We kissed goodbye. . . . It gave me great comfort to share this song from the worship service in my mother's church.

Diane was now ready to die. She had said her farewells, made plans for her body, organized her Life Celebration, and designated memorials. She had finished her work on earth.

Diane's conscious dying process did not happen by chance. It took meticulous planning and daily choices that were congruent with her and her family's deepest values. As her sister-in-law, Vanda, later said, "The most remarkable thing about Diane, and the most instructive part of her amazing life, was how she died. She talked of death and therefore let others do so. She said good-byes and heard them, and that is such a rare, rare, and wonderful gift to give to the people you care about."

For months Diane had been modeling how to approach death with grace. The moment was now at hand.

---

[16] "Shalom to You" by Elsie S. Eslinger. The United Methodist Publishing House, 1983.

Diane with daughters-in-law
Jill Stevenson and Kate Manahan

— PART TWO —

A Graceful Death

Diane's "long journey with cancer" was at an end. Her death was imminent and she was ready to die.

Diane's decision to die in her own bed, and her family's decision to forego embalming and instead care for the body at home and have the visitation there harkened back to the old ways of handling death. As we discovered, the washing of the body, dressing it, and accompanying it to the crematorium were rituals that helped family members and friends absorb the finality of Diane's earthly existence, express our love for her and each other, and let our grief be assuaged. The wake and Life Celebration were ceremonies that allowed hundreds of others to honor a person who had given so much to her family, friends, and community.

Part Two describes her death and the days immediately following. The voice of Diane is silenced with her death, but the effects of her life continued to resonate as family and friends worked with grace-filled intensity to respect her wishes. We tell each chapter from our own voices as we experienced her death.

— CHAPTER EIGHT —

The Journey Ends: Home Free

NANCY

I could hardly grasp the reality: Diane, my beloved sister-in-law, was dying.

This strong, healthy marathon runner had gone from hiking, to walking, to needing a cane, to using a wheelchair. This college professor and gifted public speaker now whispered her words. She had lost almost thirty pounds, was profoundly jaundiced, had difficulty breathing, and hurt in various places. Recently, while hugging her goodbye, I had inadvertently pressed on a tumor near her spine, and she had winced.

But the worst thing was the unrelenting itching. Two weeks before, I had offered to give her a massage, but she had asked for a vigorous body-scratch instead.

While I was scratching her legs, Diane said she loved the poem I had sent her, Mary Oliver's "In Blackwater Woods." She asked me if I would read it at her Life Celebration. We talked about it calmly, rationally, as if discussing one's own funeral were the most natural thing in the world. But on the drive back home, I howled with grief.

The evening of July 13, 2001, I was again in Mankato to see Diane. When I arrived, my brother Bill told me, "Diane's ready to die, but she doesn't know how to do it. She's so strong she could live for several days or even weeks."

Bill went upstairs with me. Diane was lying in bed, looking tired but beautiful. There were no visible signs of cancer. Kate later told me that two days earlier, after she had given Diane a bath, Diane's stylist had come to the house to wash and do her hair. As I leaned over to kiss her hello and hold her hand, I could smell her fresh warm scent.

"Diane, it's Nancy. I know it's late, but I just wanted to say hello before I go over to MaryPat and Jon's place for the night."

She nodded and squeezed my hand. I sat on the bed and tried to be an open channel for comfort and peace, letting loving energy flow toward Diane.

Bill watched us. He knew I had to leave soon. After a few minutes, he came over to the bed. She put her arms around his neck and he helped her stand up and walk to the bathroom. She sat unsupported on the toilet.

"Goodnight, Sweetie," I said from the bathroom doorway. "I'll be back in the morning."

"Okay," Diane whispered, a smile barely lifting the corners of her mouth.

Diane's sister Patt stayed until ten o'clock that evening. She told me that before she left, she leaned over the bed and said, "Goodnight, Diane. I love you." Diane whispered back, "I love you, too." Those were the last words she ever spoke.

Topher took the midnight to four a.m. shift so Bill could sleep. As he lay next to his mother, he could hear her stop breathing for a while, gasp, and then resume breathing. This pattern, called Cheyne-Stokes Respiration, is typical of someone in the dying process. At four o'clock, Topher's wife Katy relieved him.

After an early breakfast, I drove back to Bill and Diane's house. Riding with me were Tessa, who would turn four the next day, and two-year-old Teliz. On the drive, the kids practiced a song they had just learned. They belted out the Northwoods canoeing tune in their clear, piping voices.

"Can we sing this for Grandma Di-Di?" Tessa asked.

"Yes, of course," I said. "Your grandma has spent a lot of time canoeing in the wilderness. She'd probably love to hear your song."

When we arrived and climbed the stairs to the bedroom, Diane was lying on her side, her eyes closed. She seemed to be resting comfortably.

"Good morning, Katy," I said. "Good morning, Diane. It's Nancy. Tessa and Teliz are here, too."

Diane didn't respond.

"They've been practicing a song they'd like to sing for you. Would you like to hear it?"

Diane immediately pushed herself to a sitting position and swung her legs over the side of the bed. Blond-haired Tessa and Teliz stood side by side looking up at their grandmother's face and sang softly.

> Land of the silver birch
> Home of the beaver
> Where still the mighty moose
> Wanders at will.

Although Diane kept her eyes closed, she leaned toward the children and appeared to be listening intently. Their voices grew more confident:

> Blue lake and rocky shore,
> I will return once more.
> Boom-diddy-ah-da, Boom-diddy-ah-da,
> Boom-diddy-ah-da, bo-oo-oom.

After another verse, Tessa and Teliz giggled with pleasure at their performance. They scampered downstairs, calling back "Bye, Grandma Di-Di!"

Katy looked tired. She had been with Diane for almost four hours. I told her that I would take the next shift. We didn't realize it would be the last one.

Diane lay back down on her side. I joined her on the bed, my face less than a foot away. I marveled at her clear, supple skin and generous lips.

Suddenly Diane opened her eyes fully and gazed directly at me. The deep blue of her irises against the bright yellow-gold of her eyes still astonished me. During the past six weeks, I had not gotten used to what liver failure had done to her skin and eye color.

Diane kept staring at me. I started to feel uncomfortable. Did she need anything? Did she want to say something? Did she even see me? Gradually her gaze soothed my fears and answered my questions. I could see no anguish in her eyes, no suffering or sorrow. I sensed a deep, calm spaciousness, as if I were looking through her eyes into eternity. I settled down inside myself. For long, precious minutes, we just gazed and breathed together.

Then Diane pushed herself back into a sitting position and swung her legs over the side of the bed, her bare feet on the floor. I got off the bed and faced her. She reached up and pulled my head to her shoulder. I had seen Diane do this with Bill the night before when he had helped her stand and walk to the bathroom. Thinking she needed to use the bathroom again, I started to straighten up. But Diane clamped down on my neck. She *was* strong!

"Do you want me to stay like this for a while?" I asked.

She didn't respond.

I was bent almost ninety degrees at the waist. After a minute, my back was aching.

"Diane, this position isn't comfortable for me. If you want some support to stay sitting up, I could get behind you, and you could lean against me. How would that be?"

Immediately Diane's hands dropped to her lap. I crawled onto the bed behind her and pulled her snug against me so that her legs stretched out between my legs. She leaned back against my chest, her cheek touching my cheek.

For the next two and a half hours, that's how we stayed. It was one of the most intimate and sacred experiences of my life. It was an honor to hold her, support her, breathe with her, love her.

After a while, I felt words coming to me. I pushed them away. Diane didn't need to hear anything. After all, she was engaged in one of the most profound labors of her life. But the words kept coming, and eventually I trusted them. If Diane wanted me to be quiet, she would let me know.

"That's right, Diane . . . Just let yourself relax . . . I'm right here with you . . . You don't have to do anything . . . You can let go and follow the process . . ."

I sensed a little release of tension in her body. I felt calm and steady, as if I had been with a dying person many times. In fact, it was the first time.

I felt grateful for the three years of Living in Process training I had done with Anne Wilson Schaef. This self-directed healing work included hours of sitting on a mat beside someone who was allowing repressed feelings to surface, supporting them in their deep emotional release process. I had learned to trust my intuition about when to be a silent witness and when to say something encouraging or reassuring. Sitting with Diane felt similar.

"You know exactly how to do this, Di . . . Just like you knew how to be born."

I wasn't trying to think of anything to say, but from time to time, words spilled into the companionable, luminous stillness.

"Everything's going to be fine, Diane . . . *You* are going to be fine . . . In fact, you're going to be *more* than fine . . . You're going to be free of any struggle, any pain, any itching!"

I could feel her relax more deeply. We were breathing together, eyes closed, comfortable.

"You'll know when the time is right to leave. You can do it in your own time and in your own way."

I figured it would be several more days. It seemed that anyone strong enough to wrap her arms around my neck in a vice-like grip wasn't about to die.

At ten o'clock, after almost two hours, I said, "I just want to let you know that I have a half hour left to be with you. Becky is arriving at ten-thirty to drive us to Madelia for lunch with our moms. If there's anything you need before I leave, just let me know in whatever way you can."

Diane gave no response.

I resumed the rhythm of comfortable silences and the occasional words that seemed to come not so much *from* me as *through* me. I didn't even know if I believed all the words, but I felt compelled to say them.

"You're almost home, Diane . . . All those you have loved will be there to welcome you . . . your mother, your father, the baby you lost . . . They will be so happy to see you . . . Everyone is waiting for you . . . You'll be home free, Diane . . . *Home free*."

A few minutes later, Bill came upstairs. He kissed Diane's hand, looked at my position supporting her, and asked, "Are you comfortable?"

"Pretty comfortable," I replied. In truth, my back was starting to tire.

He propped pillows around me, which felt wonderful, and mentioned that Laura and Bev had said they would come between ten-thirty and eleven o'clock. He took a chair at the foot of the bed, leaned forward, and tenderly took his wife's hand.

At ten-thirty I glanced at the clock. Since there was no sign of Becky, I stayed in place, holding Diane. Our chests rose and fell together.

"That's it, Di, just trust the process. Mmm-hmm. Home free. *Home free*." It was so effortless, I felt as if I could stay with her forever.

Katy, refreshed from a nap, came back upstairs. "How's it going?"

"We're doing well," Bill said.

"I'll be leaving in a few minutes," I told her, "as soon as Becky arrives."

Katy went downstairs to ask Tim or Kate to take my place.

They both came upstairs. Tim sat down and taking his mother's right hand, put his fingers on her wrist, as he would have done with one of his patients.

"Her pulse feels thready," he said.

Kate studied Diane's face, left the bedroom and asked everyone to come upstairs. Diane was taking longer pauses between breaths.

Kate returned and started the music Diane had chosen to die to, *Bach for the Bath*. The first piece was full, slow, intense. After several measures, a plaintive cello entered.

"Oh, Diane," I said. "There's your beloved cello."

More family members had gathered around. Everyone was quiet, listening to the soaring music. Suddenly I felt Becky behind me on the bed, one hand on the center of my back, the other on Diane's arm.

As the Bach piece came to a slow, peaceful close, Tim touched his fingers to Diane's wrist again, then to her neck.

"I don't get a pulse," he said.

Everyone looked at Diane, unable to take in Tim's words.

"But she still seems to be breathing," he observed.

Diane's chest was rising and falling, slowly, steadily. After a minute, Tim touched her neck again and said, "I think that's Nancy breathing. She's gone."

It was true. She was gone.

Bill, still holding Diane's hand, put his head on their joined hands on the bed and sobbed, "Thank goodness, thank goodness." After days of yearning for death, Diane had finally been released.

Although we all were crying, I felt strangely calm, full, saturated with the sacred mystery of the moment.

"You did it, Diane," I murmured, tears running down my cheeks and wetting Diane's still warm cheek. "You really did it. You're home free."

— CHAPTER NINE —

The Ritual of Washing

NANCY

Bev and Laura arrived at the house moments after Diane died. I was still holding her when they entered the bedroom. They knelt beside the bed and burst into tears.

Diane's sister and brother-in-law, Patt and Jerry Madson, had been driving from their campground and were about ten blocks from the house when Topher reached them on their cell phone. As soon as they turned into the driveway, Patt told us later, she leapt from the truck and raced up the stairs, as if time could make a difference. When she saw Diane, still in the cotton pajamas with little rose buds, she wailed and almost collapsed. Topher put his arm around Patt to support her.

Soon Bill and Diane's oldest son Mike arrived. He had been in a meeting with landscape clients when the call came, and he extricated himself as soon as he could. Everyone was gathered around the bed or sitting on it. Bach continued to play softly in the background. At one point, someone suggested that we put on "Annie's Song," by John Denver. When the notes of the poignant ballad filled the air, many of us joined in singing one of Bill and Diane's favorite love songs. Diane did indeed "fill up" our senses. We were in a heightened state of awareness, our hearts overflowing with the mystery, beauty, and sacredness of her death.

After the tears subsided, we began discussing how we should proceed. Remembering that Diane had told Bill to do what made sense at the time of her death, he suggested holding the visitation that day since so many family members and friends were already in town. He didn't want to have Diane embalmed, nor did he want to cool her body with dry ice for a public viewing a day or two later. We would keep Diane at the house for the afternoon and take her body to the crematorium later that day. A wake could be held in two days, on Monday, giving out-of-towners a chance to get to Mankato, and her Life Celebration could take place on Tuesday. Although we regretted that people living out of state would not arrive in time to view Diane, we agreed to this plan. The four sons went downstairs to telephone other family members and friends with the news.

Bill knew that there was a finite window in which Diane's body could be prepared for a private viewing. Blood would be pooling as her body cooled, and rigor mortis would fix the joints in place. The Crossings Care Packet suggested catheterizing the bladder to prevent a natural voiding when the muscles released. Bill thought it was time to do this and to wash Diane's body.

He invited those women close to Diane to perform the ritual. (Diane had asked that women and Bill, but not her sons, care for her body.) Others were asked to leave the room. I saw Becky considering what to do and watched her reluctantly leave.

I shifted my position from behind Diane so we could lay her flat on the bed. Her three daughters-in-law, Kate, Katy, and Jill, stayed, as well as Tessa, Patt, Bev, Laura, and Bill. Bev knelt down beside Tessa and told her that they were about to start a ritual that women had performed for thousands of years for people who had died. They were going to wash Grandma Di's body and dress her in beautiful clothes.

Gently we removed Diane's pajamas. Bill placed a thick towel under her hips and inserted a catheter to drain off the urine into a sealed bag. It was surrealistic, watching him calmly and competently perform this necessary medical procedure. An unusual mixture of practical science and sacred mystery was happening before my eyes, and I found it wonderful that Diane's beloved husband, Bill, and not a mortician, was the one touching Diane's body.

As Bill tucked the still-attached catheter bag out of sight under the towel, Kate brought a large ceramic bowl made by Diane's friend, John Glick, filled it with warm water and stirred in lavender oil, a fragrance used for millennia in bathwater.[17]

The nine of us had never done this before, but we seemed to fall into our roles effortlessly, positioning ourselves around Diane. I knelt by her leg.

I had often read novels or seen movies in which women washed the body of a family member, but I had never envisioned myself doing it. I felt a little tentative but still in an altered state of consciousness in which everything flowed easily.

Kate dipped a washcloth in the scented water, wrung it out, and handed it to Bill, who was kneeling at Diane's head. She handed a second cloth to Patt, by Diane's shoulder. When Bill finished cleaning Diane's face, he gave the cloth back to Kate, who rinsed it out, gave it to the next person, and so on. Each person wiped a different part of Diane's body, including four-year-old Tessa, who washed her grandmother's stomach. Laura washed Diane's ankles and feet in memory of all the walking and hiking they had done together. I washed her right thigh, which felt muscular and supple.

After tipping her from side to side to clean her back, we patted her dry with a towel. Kate invited everyone to say whatever was in our hearts. I have no memory of what I or anyone else said. All I remember is that the room felt like a temple filled with love.

As the ritual ended, we wondered what to do with the water left in the bowl. It didn't feel right to pour it down the drain. Kate suggested that it nourish Diane's flower garden. So she and Jill carried the heavy bowl downstairs and out the back door to the children's

---

[17] The Romans believed lavender represented purity. The word "lavender" comes from *lavo*, the Latin word for "wash."

garden, where they cast handfuls of water, pungent with lavender, into the air. It rained down on the flowers and soaked into the earth.

Back upstairs, Laura went to the closet for the outfit Diane had specified: a navy blue skirt, a short-sleeved white blouse, a navy vest, and the blue dress shoes Patt and Diane had bought earlier that year for a wedding Diane had hoped to attend.

While the others dressed Diane, I went downstairs, where Becky was serving curried chicken, Indian rice, and vegetables. I was grateful for the familiar home-cooked food. When my nephews finished eating, they got back on their cell phones.

After eating, I went back upstairs. Diane was dressed, and Laura was putting a pillow under her head. Patt crossed Diane's legs at the ankle so her feet would not splay, and Kate swirled a white silk shroud, also from the Crossings Care Packet, over her legs, concealing the catheter bag taped to her thigh. Bev and Laura applied Diane's usual lipstick and combed her hair. We put away any clinical items, lit candles on the dresser, and opened the window to let in fresh air. Little Tessa performed the sacred ritual of smudging by carrying lit herbal sage slowly around the bedroom, sweeping aromatic smoke into each area and around Diane's body.

Bill told Becky and me that washing Diane's body after she died "was the most sacred thing" he had ever done. My brother said he felt close to Diane, that "her soul was still there." The experience was so profound that it eased his grief.

I had a similar experience. My initial uncertainties dissolved in the rightness and sacredness of this ancient ritual. Washing Diane's body with my brother, family members, and her closest friends not only comforted me but, I believe, helped surround Diane with love and support as she transitioned to the next realm.

Sue Towey, Laura Turk, Diane, Mary Lofy, and Bev Palmquist
August 3, 1996

— CHAPTER TEN —

The Viewing

BECKY

While Diane's body was being washed, I heated up the Indian food I had brought from home. I sat at the kitchen table with Bill and Diane's sons as they took a break from letting people know about their mother's death and the viewing being held that very day. Later in the afternoon she would be taken to the crematorium, so this would be the only chance to see her.

Once Diane's body had been dressed and the room cleaned up, the bedroom door was opened for the visitation. Silently, the family and friends who were gathered downstairs filed in. The scene was beautiful. Diane was tastefully dressed, and the swirl of silk over her legs had an artistic flair that seemed true to her spirit.

The room was peaceful, with candles burning on the dresser and soft music playing in the background. A big bouquet of daisies—a birthday present to Patt from her daughter, Pam—sat on the bedside table. A few folding chairs were nearby for those who could not stand for long. The room was not air-conditioned and felt hot, even with the window open, so we brought in a fan.

For the next four hours, friends and family streamed through the bedroom. Diane's brother-in-law, Jim Manahan, arrived with his two teen-aged grandchildren visiting from Singapore. His wife, Vanda, scooped up the smallest children and drove them to Madelia, Diane's home town, for the annual Madelia Days parade. I admired her thoughtfulness at getting the children out of the house and giving them something fun to do. I also thought how appropriate it was that the streets of Diane's home town were lined with flags and celebrants, as if cheering her on.

One of the most touching moments was when Diane's mother-in-law arrived from Madelia. When Ruth entered the room and saw Diane, her face crumpled. Weeping softly, Ruth sat next to the bed and held Diane's hand, which bore the diamond ring she had given her two months earlier.

Diane's friends Chuck and Mary Lofy arrived from Minneapolis. When Mary saw Diane on the bed, she knelt and sobbed on Diane's chest. Tears streamed freely down Chuck's face. Their tears let loose the floodgates for others.

As the hours of visitation neared the end, Patt removed Ruth's ring from Diane's finger and gave it back to Ruth. Kate played "Annie's Song" again. Most joined in, the tears welling up for many. Bill, his voice cracking, sang the love song to his wife for the last time.

The mortician was to arrive at 4:30. By that time, all the people who could make it to Mankato had arrived. One by one, they took a moment to be with Diane and say a final farewell. I kissed her forehead, and said good-bye.

It was time for Diane's body to leave.

Patt Madson with her sister, Diane, 1999

— CHAPTER ELEVEN —

The Cremation

NANCY

Hank Kolbinger, the mortician, drove the hearse up the driveway promptly at 4:30. I shuddered as I heard him coming up the stairs. He greeted us with kindness and reviewed the procedure for removing Diane's body.

Bill slipped off Diane's remaining jewelry. Hank spread out a white sheet next to Diane, and he and Bill lifted her onto it. He tucked the sheet around her so she was tightly wrapped. Only the very top of her head—her lustrous silver hair—was visible.

Kate couldn't bear the silence. She opened a drawer marked "Classical," pulled out a compact disc at random, and put it on. The music was powerful and stirring. She noticed later that it was Mozart's *Requiem*, a mass for the dead, composed as Mozart himself lay on his deathbed.

To the strains of this poignant lament, Bill and Diane's sons—Mike, Dave, Tim, and Topher—lifted their mother's shrouded body from the bed and carried it out to the hall.

Their feet spoke of their distinct personalities: Mike wore work boots, Dave was barefooted, Tim had on Tevas, and Topher's feet were in clogs. But they worked together as if they had done it before, carefully turning the corner, gracefully stepping down the wide carpeted stairs, slowing passing through the front doorway, and gently placing their mother on the waiting gurney.

The boys wheeled Diane down the cement walkway to the hearse in the driveway. Her dearest friends, Laura, Bev, Mary, and Sue lined the walk, like an honor guard. About thirty other friends, family members, and neighbors, joined the column to see Diane off. One-year-old Owen, Tim and Kate's son, solemnly waved "bye-bye" as his grandmother passed by, a gesture he had just learned.

As had been decided beforehand, Diane would not be left alone. Bill, Tim, and Kate stayed home to look after houseguests and others who had come for the visitation and to start making arrangements for the wake and Life Celebration. I offered to go to the crematorium with David, Jill, Topher, and Katy. After accompanying Diane through her dying, I wanted to stay beside her for the whole journey. After saying good-bye to Becky, who was returning to Minneapolis, I joined David in the hearse for the ride to the funeral home. Topher, Katy, and Jill followed in Bill's car.

At the mortuary, Hank and an assistant transferred Diane's body to a stiff cardboard box. Before Hank put on the lid, I bent to kiss her forehead.

"Don't touch the body!" he cried.

"Why not?" I said, taken aback.

"Well," he said, "there's bacteria. We're dealing with a body here. You should all wash your hands thoroughly. The bathroom's right over there."

I was speechless. This was Diane, whose body we had bathed, whose hands people had been holding all afternoon. She wasn't just "a body." I almost didn't go to the bathroom out of principle, but I wanted to use it before the hundred-mile trip to the crematorium. Those moments alone gave me the opportunity to let go of my anger, remember that it's a good idea to wash your hands in any situation, and acknowledge that Hank was simply being a conscientious mortician.

By the time I emerged from the bathroom, the box was in the

hearse. I resumed my place beside the driver. Dave sat behind us. The coffin was in a separate compartment in back. Jill, Topher, and Katy again followed in Bill's car. Our little caravan left Mankato, heading northwest one hundred miles to Echo, Minnesota, and the crematorium the mortuary used.

The driver tried to strike up a conversation.

"So, how're we doin' today?" he said cheerfully.

"We're all right," Dave and I murmured.

"So then, did you know the deceased?"

David spoke from the back seat. "She's my mother."

"Oh, so how did she die, was it sudden-like, or had she been ill for a long time?"

"She died of breast cancer six hours ago," I replied.

"Well, I'm sure sorry to hear that," he said. "So what did she do?"

"Actually, we're still grieving," I said. "We're not much in the mood to talk."

"Oh, well, I didn't mean to pry. It's just that I'm not used to anyone riding with me. In fact this is the first time I've ever had anyone come along—well, except for the deceased, of course, heh, heh."

We thanked him for understanding. True to his word, the driver didn't question us again. Eventually Dave and I softly conversed.

After two hours, we arrived at a square metal building, one of the few crematoria in Southern Minnesota at that time. A field of corn shimmered nearby in the dying July light.

The owner of the Echo Funeral Home and crematorium, mortician Tim Kurlow, met us at the door. He looked healthy, relaxed, and comfortable in his gray slacks and short-sleeved deep blue shirt. The driver wheeled in the box and left for his solitary return trip to Mankato.

Mr. Kurlow's demeanor was professional but cheerful, matter-of-fact but compassionate. He welcomed us warmly and explained the cremation process with a good mixture of technical and layperson's language. We were standing in a spacious, clean room in front of a large free-standing furnace, which he called a cremation chamber. I studied the control panel's knobs, dials and temperature gauges. Mr. Kurlow said that it would take two hours for a body the size of Diane's to burn. The furnace needed to reach sixteen hundred degrees, consume the body, and cool down for another couple of hours. Then the ashes—he called them *cremains*—would be removed from the chamber.

When the mortician invited our questions, I asked how common it was for a family to accompany the body. Mr. Kurlow said that in his eleven years of running the crematorium, we were the only white family to do so. Laotian and Hmong families had come with their loved ones, he explained. They and the Buddhist monks placed reeds and flowers on the box before it went into the crematory chamber. Because Buddhists believe that smoke carries the spirit to heaven, the families would wait to see the smoke rising from the chimney. Since state law requires a hundred percent burn of a body with no fumes, Mr. Kurlow would allow smoke from the burning reeds and flowers to escape. As soon as the Buddhist children who were gathered outside the crematorium saw smoke rising from the chimney, they threw coins from baskets into the air so the spirit would have money for its journey.

When Dave asked to have the box opened so we could say our final good-bye, Mr. Kurlow didn't hesitate before lifting the cover. Diane looked peaceful. In fact, a little smile had raised the corners of her mouth during the trip across the prairie. We gazed at her face for the last time, and I kissed her forehead. After the cover was replaced, we all guided the box as it slid on rollers into the cold cremation chamber.

Mr. Kurlow shut the door securely. We took a collective breath while he pushed the button to start the flames.

"Do you want to see the skeletal remains before I remove them from the chamber?" he asked. "Often the skeleton is relatively intact as the larger bones don't burn completely."

We looked at each other, aghast. We hadn't anticipated that option. Did we really want to see Diane's skeleton?

Gradually, we overcame our initial discomfort, and one by one, nodded our heads. We had accompanied Diane this far. Why shrink from witnessing her transformation all the way?

"Yes, we'd like that. Thank you for offering,"

"In that case, you can return at ten-thirty, when the cremains should be cool enough to be removed from the chamber," Mr. Kurlow said. "I'm sorry there's not much to do in town, but The Recovery Room down on Main Street is probably open if you'd like a bite to eat."

David, Jill, Topher, Katy, and I stood outside the door of the crematorium. It was a balmy summer evening with just a little breeze. We walked the few blocks to Main Street, where the stores were locked, but the aptly-named restaurant was open. A few locals were at the bar watching a ballgame.

After we had ordered hamburgers, I excused myself and went outside. I needed a few minutes alone to absorb what had happened. I had started out the day expecting to visit Diane, meet Becky, have lunch with our mothers, and be back in Minneapolis by now. I had ended up miles away from home in a little prairie town as Diane's body was being consumed by flames.

I reached the Echo city park and walked toward a row of trees. I looked back to see if any smoke was rising from the crematorium, but I couldn't see the chimney in the dark. The huge oaks and cottonwoods were solidly rooted in the ground, yet their branches swayed and their leaves rustled in the night breeze. I prayed for some of their quiet strength and graceful flexibility for myself, for Diane's family, and for her friends, colleagues and students. I prayed for everyone in the world who was dying that night and for their loved ones.

I whispered, "And we drop like the fruits of the tree. Even we. Even so." I remembered sharing those final lines from George Meredith's poem "Dirge in Woods" a few months earlier while Diane and I were walking in Sibley Park. She asked to hear them again and chuckled at Meredith's rueful humor, reminding us that we are not the center of the universe and that we have about as much control over our dropping as does a peach. But also, like the peach, we are part of the ongoing cycle of life.

Comforted and calmed, I walked back to The Recovery Room, where my nephews and their wives had just been served. Rarely has a juicy hamburger tasted so wonderful. The pitcher of icy beer helped revive us, too.

Later we wandered through Echo, eventually coming to an open church. We sat in the dark pews, resting. Dave and Topher soon spotted a door to the basement, where they discovered a ping-pong table. They called up for the rest of us to come and see. We turned on the lights, and after some discussion about how appropriate it would be to play a game while their mother was being cremated just down the street—shouldn't we be acting more reverent, more sorrowful, more grown-up?—we picked up the ping-pong paddles. We realized that Diane, a child at heart, would be delighted we had found a way to have fun on this of all nights. What better tribute to a woman who managed to be playful while doing just about everything!

At ten-thirty we returned to the crematorium. The oven had cooled down, and Mr. Kurlow was opening the door. We peered in and saw, amidst the jumble of ashes, Diane's bones. The mortician pointed out her thigh and upper arms, as well as her pelvis and skull. Seeing Diane's bare bones felt eerie and miraculous, impossible and inevitable, like a dream.

But it wasn't a dream. Mr. Kurlow matter-of-factly fetched a long-handled steel broom, donned heavy gloves, and swept the bones and ashes down a chute at the front of the chamber into a metal pan. He carried the pan over to the adjacent work area, where he stirred the ashes with a giant U-shaped magnet. Dozens of staples from the cardboard box clumped on to both ends of the magnet, and the metal arch supports from Diane's high-heeled shoes dangled from one side. Mr. Kurlow discarded the steel items and reached in for Diane's titanium hip joint.

Then he placed the cremains into a large, industrial-strength blender, flipped the switch, and waited while the bones and teeth were pulverized and mixed with the ashes. After allowing the dust to settle, he removed the cover and poured the resulting gray grit into a plastic bag, secured the bag, and took it to the redwood box Topher had made. I could see Topher holding his breath. The bag was larger than we had anticipated. Mr. Kurlow pressed it down into the box. It fit perfectly.

With the box in hand, along with the artificial hip and documentation from the mortuary, we drove back to Mankato, arriving at one a.m. Bill was sitting at the kitchen table waiting for us. He was exhausted from the long, intense day, from communicating with dozens of friends and family members, and from taking care of practical matters. Still, he looked calm and at peace.

We placed the box of ashes and Diane's artificial hip on the table in front of him. He opened the box, took out the bag of ashes, and held it quietly in both hands. After several moments, still holding Diane's ashes, he asked about the trip and listened intently as the five of us shared our experiences. He laughed with delight when we told him about playing ping pong while Diane was being cremated, something he knew she would have loved us doing.

I was too tired to drive back to my niece's house for the night, so I slept on Bill and Di's porch, just off the kitchen. Bill gave me a toothbrush and Diane's flannel rosebud pajamas, which he had washed and dried while we were at the crematorium. I put them on and went to bed on the porch sofa.

Even though the journey had been long and difficult, I was glad I had gone. By accompanying Diane's body to the crematorium and bringing her ashes back home, I had shifted to the next stage of grieving. David and Topher told me later that it was during the drive to and from Echo that they were able to let go of their mother. Katy and Jill said that the trip completed the whole cycle of Diane's death for them and made it seem more natural.

As I drifted off to sleep, Diane's soft flannel pajamas both eerily and comfortingly familiar against my skin, I knew what they meant.

> Like the fruit of the tree.
> Even we.
> Even so.

— CHAPTER TWELVE —

The Wake

BECKY

On Monday evening, two days after Diane died, I returned to Mankato with clean clothes for Nancy in time for the seven p.m. wake at Bill and Diane's home. It was an opportunity for the extended family and intimate friends to remember her, to tell stories, to laugh, and to shed tears.

Tim and Topher blew steadily into their didgeridoos, the four-foot-long musical pipes of the Australian aborigines, to summon the milling group. Over thirty people made their way to the large wooden deck and arranged their chairs in a circle as the deep tones reverberated across the backyard.

It had been another hot summer day and at seven o'clock, the air was still muggy. Diane's mother-in-law, Ruth Manahan, sat between Nancy and me. We faced the unfenced back yards that formed a long, green expanse of neatly mown lawns. Behind the yard was a ravine where maple trees and cottonwoods rustled in the breeze. The box with Diane's ashes rested on a table along with several framed pictures of her.

Bill welcomed everyone and invited us to share our memories of Diane or any thoughts, feelings, poems, or songs. His voice was hoarse, moving toward the laryngitis he would develop by the next day. The faces of the immediate family revealed an exhaustion born from loss, relief, adrenaline, constant interacting with people, long to-do lists, and lack of sleep. We sat in silence for a few moments.

Laura Turk rose. She reflected on the miles she and Diane had walked over the years (she calculated at least twelve thousand since 1975) and over all those miles, they had talked, shared secrets, and supported each other in times of struggle and pain as well as accomplishment and joy. Laura told of a time when they visited Sister Ramona, a nun in Mankato, for a spiritual consultation. The nun told Diane, "God gives us grace to give, but will give you a tremendous grace to receive." And, indeed, as Laura pointed out, for all that Diane had given to others, when her time of need came, the outpouring was tremendous. Laura ended her reflection by passing around a box of embroidered handkerchiefs she had bought at an antique store. It was a touching gift that many of us put to use.

One by one, as they felt moved, people rose and spoke. Chuck Lofy read a letter he had written to Tessa, explaining why her grandmother had been such a special person.[18] Bill's nieces, Betsy and Katie Anderson, performed "All God's Children Just Love to Dance," a whimsical song that Diane had asked them to sing for her. As they opened with the line, "I bet you a kangaroo we could all dance to a didgeridoo," smiles broke out as we recalled Diane's love of fun.

Tim talked about what a wise mother Diane was. When the boys were young, pandemonium often seemed to reign in the house. One day, Diane took a couple of the boys on a walk and said, "What's going on with you guys?" Tim told her they were mad because their dad wasn't around enough. A few weeks later, Bill started spending half an hour each evening with the boy whose turn it was to wash the dishes. Often they would just play catch. Tim felt like it was a turning point in the family dynamics. His mother had listened to them and figured out what to do. Bill piped up, "I always thought that brilliant idea was mine!" It was a classic example of how Diane

[18] See "Appendix D: An Open Letter to Tessa Manahan from Chuck Lofy" for a copy of the letter.

could prompt people to do what was needed—and sometimes even let them take the credit for it!

Diane's strength was another theme of the wake. Close friend Susie Symons told of a time in 1975 when she was at the Manahan home having dinner. The phone rang. It was one of Diane's therapy clients. Diane listened for a moment and then said, "Did you want to ask me if this is a good time to talk?" A long pause followed. "Seven-thirty would be good." Susie was shocked to see a woman set clear boundaries, communicate firmly yet diplomatically, and provide a gentle lesson to another. She summed up Diane's gift: "Her intensity, beauty, and grace made me come alive. She brought out the depth, beauty, and finest we can be."

Jon Olseth added to that sentiment. He told of how Diane invited him to her holistic nursing class each year to teach poetry. Diane wanted her students to experience the music of language. She told him, "I love how words feel, the resonance that lingers after a poem is done." Jon said, "I feel the same way about Diane. We can still feel her resonance, her poetry and beauty and grace."

Of course, a recurring theme of the evening was how much Diane would be missed. John Lofy, who had flown in from Ann Arbor, said that he first met Diane thirty years earlier when he was a boy:

> Diane was the most glamorous woman I'd ever met. I adored her. Later, I looked to Bill and Diane as role models for marriage—they traveled and had adventures, their love was solid. It made me believe that marriage and adventure [weren't mutually exclusive].

John married a wonderful woman and started a family. Two months before Diane died, he took his family on their first camping trip in Utah. One night he dreamed that his three-year-old son was in an airport terminal walking away from him. His wife told him to let the boy go on his own, and as he watched the receding figure, it was as if he were seeing his boy grow up without him.

> I was filled with such sorrow at how we meet each other

> and get to know each other . . . and how we are always walking away from each other. When I woke, I called my parents and apologized for not being three years old any more and I wrote a letter to Diane saying I'm sorry, I'm sorry, I'm sorry that you have to go on without us and that we have to go on without you . . . I wish life were different . . . The only consolation is that because time passes, we get to know more people and we get to love more people.

Stunned by John's eloquence, many of us teared up. Bill rose and hugged him.

By now the light was waning and the breeze had picked up, providing some relief from the heat. The voice of the cicadas rose and fell in the background. Nancy rose to speak:

> Bill met Diane fifty years ago, which means that I too have known Di for fifty years. Diane played drums in the high school band, something ordinary girls didn't do in the 1950s. She inspired me to become a drummer, too. I happened to get the band uniform she had worn, and every time I put on the jacket, I felt a secret thrill at seeing her initials penned inside the collar . . . I was lucky to have stayed with Bill and Diane for weeks or months at a time, in Hawaii, in Oklahoma, and in Ghana helping to care for the children. Diane taught me to love West African culture. We studied tribal art, shopped in open air markets, and wore dresses made by her local dressmaker. But it was the talks before and after our almost daily, very competitive, tennis matches that cemented our friendship.
>
> Diane showed her support for me as a lesbian in so many ways. She and Bill donated money to organizations working for gay civil rights, she wrote letters to the editor, and she counseled parents going through a child's coming out. When I fell in love with Becky, Diane was almost as thrilled as I was. She celebrated happiness with the verve of someone who was intensely in love with life. One anniversary, she gave Becky and me an alabaster

> statue of two graceful, androgynous figures in an open-hearted embrace. We keep this statue on our living room mantle, a continuous reminder of Diane's love. I will miss her terribly.

The lights in the neighborhood came on and a warm yellow light filled the back hallway. All the Manahan grandchildren were inside, the younger ones now being put down for the night. Laura spoke once more:

> A few years ago, Diane asked me to go to St. Peter to sing in the Messiah with her and, despite the fact that I wasn't much of a singer, it was a highlight. Three days before she died, Bev and I were with her for an hour and a half. We thought we'd sing something from the Messiah, knowing how much Diane loved the music. She was in and out of sleep . . . We got to the words "Wonderful, Counselor, Almighty God, the Everlasting Power, the Prince of Peace." Diane opened her eyes and said, "*GET THE TAPE.*"

We laughed. That sounded so much like Diane. Even on her deathbed, she could be clear and direct. Laura continued:

> So the next day I brought the CD. She was kind of out of it, but when the Messiah started playing, she raised her hand from the bed and with one finger, directed the chorus.

Everyone was silent as the evening darkened into night, waiting to see if anyone else would rise.

At last, Pam Prather, Diane's only niece, stood and spoke the final words. Her voice quavered. "The core of Diane was love, peace, and harmony. Whoever knew her was graced by her. All her memories are blessings."

Everyone went home or to stay with family or friends. We all needed to rest and prepare for the next day's final tribute to Diane.

— CHAPTER THIRTEEN —

The Life Celebration

NANCY

As Diane wished, her Life Celebration was held in Mankato's Sibley Park, where she had spent so much time over the years walking in solitude or with company. This was the event she had spent weeks planning in detail. She had arranged the speakers, chosen the music and musicians, composed the text for a bookmark, and delegated dozens of chores. She was not in the least embarrassed about claiming a final tribute. As I had heard Diane unapologetically explain, "I deserve it!"

That Tuesday, July 18, 2001, was one of the hottest days of the year, with the temperature approaching one hundred degrees. The heat did not keep people away, however; nearly four hundred attended Diane's celebration.

Each person was given the bookmark Diane had designed as "a little something" for those who attended her celebration. On one side was a graceful, vibrant iris, drawn by her friend John Glick. On the other side were the words Diane had written for the occasion.[19]

---

[19] See page 109 for the text of Diane's bookmark.

The printed programs were a collaborative effort: the layout was by Bill and Diane's son Mike, a front page poem was by their son Dave, pen and ink drawings of dancing African women were by Dave's wife Jill, and a back page obituary was by John Lofy. It listed Diane's seventeen "life bearers" (rather than pall bearers) and her twelve best friends from St. Olaf College, almost all of whom were there.

A podium draped with two Nepalese prayer shawls, one white and the other gold, stood in the middle of the band shell stage, surrounded by large sprays of flowers. In front of the stage, the box of Diane's cremains rested on a table along with four candles. The large candle represented Diane; three smaller ones represented the three generations Diane had touched. Eight streamers, made from the hundreds of cards Diane had received over her cancer years, ran up the sides of the band shell. Kate told me she had discovered the cards in a chest of drawers. Diane had admitted to Kate that she could never bring herself to throw them away and hoped they could be used for something.

Nearby hung a prayer flag or "Tibetan wind horse," ready for the cotton squares on which people could write memories, tributes, or just their names. Later this prayer flag was put in the garden in back of Bill and Diane's house for the messages to flutter around the home and yard and beyond. I wrote simply "Home Free. Love, Nancy" and attached my little cloth to the line beside the other messages.

Easels held photographs of Diane that she herself had selected. Becky and I walked around looking at these pictures. Becky had on the moss-green silk suit Diane had given her. I wore a red linen dress, one of the exquisite hand-me-downs Diane had passed on to me as her weight changed over the years. Almost no one, we noticed, was wearing the traditional funeral black.

Suddenly, I felt the atmosphere shift. A deep sound sent reverberations through my body. I turned toward the source—Topher playing the didgeridoo. The haunting, pulsing tone hushed the crowd, drew everyone to the seating area, and signaled the beginning of the program.

Tom Giles, Bev Palmquist's son-in-law, started the ceremony by playing a Bach violin cantata. Toward the end of the piece, one of his strings snapped. There was an audible gasp from those who had received Diane's e-mail about Itzhak Perlman. Instead of stopping to restring his violin, Tom improvised as best he could, finishing the piece on three strings, just as Perlman had done. He hadn't received Diane's e-mail and later revealed that never before in his years of playing the violin had a string broken during a performance. It seemed as if Diane were there, overseeing the celebration she had so carefully orchestrated.

John Lofy and his sister Annmarie Rubin stepped to the microphone. John explained that we were gathered "to celebrate who Diane was and to honor what she did." He said that he and Annmarie had been surprised when Diane asked them to lead the event. But, John said, "Diane relished the idea of having the next generation usher her into the next life. She liked surprising everybody."

Annmarie observed, "Diane was clear about who she was and always curious and supportive about who others were." She summed up Diane's spirit: "She created a space around her where all senses were heightened . . . [where] life seemed less like a freight train and more like a river."

As John and Annmarie left the stage, Diane's sister Patt Madson ascended the steps with her family—husband Jerry and children Pam and Mark. Patt stepped to the podium and asked, "How in the world do you say goodbye to your only sister, your only sibling?" She didn't try to answer that wrenching question but simply remembered watching Diane grow from toddler to woman, wife, mother, and beloved aunt to their children. Patt said that after the death of their parents, she and Diane made a commitment to spend special time together each year. "Diane was loving, fun, so very funny, and she had an incredible gift of wisdom and guidance."

Patt ended by reading a poem she had seen in a recent nursing journal:

> Some people come into our lives and quickly go.
> Some people move our souls to dance.

> They awaken us to new understanding
> with the passing whisper of their wisdom.
> Some people make the sky
> more beautiful to gaze upon.
> They stay in our lives for awhile,
> Leave footprints in our hearts,

Patt's voice wavered at that line, but she regained control and spoke the final poignant line:

> And we are never, ever the same.[20]

Then my nephew walked up onto the stage and unfolded a piece of paper. "I am David," he began. "Diane's son." He took a ragged breath. "I didn't realize how hard this would be." He stepped back from the podium, took a deeper breath, and wiped his eyes.

Bill, sitting in front of me, put his face in his hands. His shoulders shook. I thought he was sobbing, but when he turned to whisper to Topher, I realized he was laughing! They both were shaking with suppressed laughter! Bill said later that he and the boys knew when Dave offered to speak for the family that he wouldn't get far without breaking down, even though David was adamant that he could do it, no problem.

"Being as I'm the only member of the immediate family speaking today . . ." He choked again.

David's wife, Jill, joined him at the podium, put her arm around him, and offered to read his remarks. David shook his head and tried again:

> I thought I'd speak about Diane as a mom. I want to speak to her. So hi, Mom. Ever since we were little, we knew you were a great mother. How did we know? You let us run around the house full speed, screaming, and naked. You let us build an obstacle course in the basement. You fought for TV rights. You allowed us to eat ice cream before dinner.

[20] C. Flavia's Legacy, LLC, used with special permission from the Flavia Company, Inc/Flavia's Legacy, LLC.

As the crowd laughed, David's voice grew stronger.

> I appreciate how you modeled grace, intelligence, playfulness, honesty. How you empowered us to believe in ourselves, in people, the earth, equality, in the truth. How you demonstrated justice and fairness through your service to others. And most of all, how you so enjoyed life, extracting the treasures of each day and freely sharing those same treasures with us, your family.

He and Jill, arms around each other's waists, walked back to their seats. I was moved by David's words. Having witnessed Diane interacting with the children for over three decades, I knew David was right. I reflected on another trait that made Diane a great mom: her ability to take lightly not only the "rules" of parenting (like No Dessert Before Meals), but also her own shortcomings as a mother. She trusted that, despite occasional parenting missteps, the boys would turn out exactly as they were meant to be.

After David finished, the head of the university's school of nursing spoke of Diane as an exceptional nurse and innovative teacher—"students flocked to her holistic nursing courses." Mary Huntley described the gathering of the school of nursing on July 3, eleven days earlier. As usual, Diane had followed her four life principles. First, she had managed to *show up* for the meeting, despite not feeling well that day. Second, she took the time to *pay attention* to what was meaningful to her colleagues and to herself. Third, Mary said, Diane was able to *tell the truth* about her condition, and about her sadness at "not being able to continue her life because she loved her life, Bill, her family, her friends." Finally, Diane had asked if her colleagues would sit together at her Life Celebration, acknowledging that of course, they might choose not to, thus *letting go of the outcome.*

Mary paused and looked out over the hundreds of people gathered to remember Diane. "In fact," she observed, "her nursing colleagues are here today, sitting together." Mary concluded by announcing that the faculty had nominated Diane for the Nurse Educator of the

Year Award. (Four months later, The Minnesota Association of Colleges of Nursing named Diane Nurse Educator of 2001.)

Susie Symons delivered a stirring eulogy that spoke of her and Diane's thirty-year friendship, and Jon Olseth performed the song he had written for Diane.[21]

One of Diane's last students, Angie Ubongen, took the podium during the open mike portion of the event. "I'm really nervous," she said. With a barely audible voice, Angie began her story:

> A few weeks ago, I was terrified about the requirement to give an oral report on our final project in front of the class. I went to Diane's office and told her about my fear of public speaking. Diane asked if I had my report with me. I did. Could I read it to her right there? So I just read it, no problem. Diane said it was excellent and suggested that when the time came, I should get into the half of the class she was supervising for the reports. I could look at her and know that I had already done this.

With Diane's encouragement, Angie survived her first public speaking. Now, only weeks later, she was doing the unimaginable: speaking in front of four hundred people in order to pay tribute to her "most wonderful teacher."

Diane's nursing colleague, Mary Johnson, told of the time she and Diane were to give a talk on holistic nursing at a conference in Orlando. Months before the conference, Diane asked if Mary would learn how to yodel with her, so they did. At the presentation, they showed a big slide of a beautiful mountain and entered from opposite corners of the room, yodeling. Mary wasn't sure what the nursing professors thought, but she and Diane had fun. Mary then broke into a trilling "yodel-odel-laydee-hoo" to honor Diane's playful spirit and to fulfill a promise to yodel at her Life Celebration.

After the last of the speakers had descended from the open microphone, Diane's "life bearers"—Bev, Laura, Mary, and Sue, her

---

[21] The eulogy and the song lyrics are reprinted in Appendices E and F respectively.

four closest friends—picked up the box of ashes, and carried it across the grassy field and up a hill. The box could have been carried by one person, but Diane had asked her friends to do this last act for her together. With grief written all over their faces, they set her box down on the high bank overlooking the Blue Earth River.

Diane's yodeling colleague invited us to sing the beautiful hymn "Morning Has Broken" popularized by Cat Stevens. The lyrics blurred on the piece of paper in my hand.

> Praise for the singing
> Praise for the morning
> Praise for their springing
> Fresh from the Earth.

I was struck by Diane's choosing a song of such elation for her funeral. She must have imagined us all gathered on the riverbank beside her ashes singing lines that expressed the core of her spiritual life: a profound, grateful, joyful connection with the cycles of nature and the miracle of the universe.

After my sister Pat and her daughters sang *Dona Nobis Pachem*, Latin for "Give Us Peace," I did what Diane had asked. I read Mary Oliver's "In Blackwater Woods," a poem about what living requires from us. At the last lines, my voice broke. Bill stepped to my side and put his hand on my shoulder. My brother's loving support helped me finish the lines about knowing when it is time to let go of your life and then . . . letting go.

Bill stepped over to the cage of homing pigeons. Diane had intended that these "doves" would represent peace and spirit, and also our letting go of her. Crouching down, Bill unlatched the door and opened it wide. The pure white birds hesitated a moment and then all seven leapt into the air, swooping out over the river. The birds quickly winged out of sight around a bend in the river, following their instinct . . . straight home.

~

Diane's tapestry was complete, with the final threads tied and cut by those who loved her. She had consciously created the ending she desired: dying at home, having her body tended by her intimate circle, creating special remembrances for family, friends, and community, and directing her own life celebration. By sharing in her journey, our own life tapestries would now contain threads of Diane woven in tightly. In every thread, grace exists.

The text Diane wrote for the bookmark distributed at her Life Celebration:

DIANE MANAHAN
August 6, 1940
July 14, 2001

My intention is to
Live out in full color
Live with passion,
Ignite ideas, laughter, wonder
And kindness
Spreading hope in times of darkness.

I know that human nature is noble,
Tender, longing and striving,
We are all connected.

My ideal of living the conscious life
Is articulated by Diane Ackerman's poem:
"...I swear I will not dishonor
my soul with hatred,
but offer myself humbly
as a guardian of nature,
as a healer of misery,
as a messenger of wonder,
as an architect of peace..."[22]

Thank you for honoring me
By your presence and spirit today.
It is time to celebrate all of life.

Summer 2001

---

[22] From *I Praise My Destroyer* by Diane Ackerman, copyright © 1998 by Diane Ackerman. Used by permission of Random House, Inc.

— PART THREE —

Living On

Diane had died, but for many people, her spirit lived on—in their memories, in the course of their lives that she had helped shape, in her published and unpublished writings, in the community work she had done, and through the memorials she had left.

For others, however, her living on had a more literal meaning.

Many people have experienced after-death communication with departed friends or family members. These are often powerful encounters that provide comforting messages and bring relief from agonizing grief. Yet, people rarely speak about these experiences because they carry a certain stigma. Western cultural does not acknowledge such communications, and their anecdotal nature renders them unscientific. We, however, are open to the continuing life of the spirit and present the following six stories about Diane's soul journey.

The first story takes us back to the moment of Diane's death with her family gathered around her. While it does not involve communication with her spirit, it indicates the passage a soul may travel.

The five stories that follow it recount after-death communication with Diane. Powerful and intimate, they describe four types of interactions: olfactory (smell), full visual appearances, sleep-state encounters, and a sense of her presence. All happened spontaneously and unexpectedly.

We are grateful to those who allowed us to share their experiences. The common threads in these encounters were the warp and woof of Diane's life tapestry: teaching and healing. These communications offer glimpses of the other side and indicate that death is not the end, but rather the doorway to a different way of being . . . and that the door is not tightly closed.

Diane Jansen Manahan
August 6, 1940 – July 14, 2001

— CHAPTER FOURTEEN —

The Portal

BECKY

On Saturday morning, July 14, 2001, I was due in Mankato at ten thirty to pick up Nancy where she had been spending time with Diane. We had planned to drive to Madelia, twenty-five miles away, to take our mothers to lunch at eleven o'clock.

But I procrastinated. I puttered around, straightened up the desk, searched for the car keys, and organized my fanny pack. Something was dragging on me. My usual need for punctuality was oddly absent.

By the time I left Minneapolis, I knew I'd be late. But the words of Nancy's motto, "Trust the process," began to play in my head, and I relaxed. So what if I arrived a little late?

As it turned out, I reached Bill and Diane's house at 10:40. Ten minutes late. Big deal, I thought, as I pulled up to the house and saw David and Jill sitting on the front steps. I waved and entered through the side porch, carrying in an Indian meal that Nancy and I had cooked for the family the day before.

But those extra ten minutes were a big deal. They gave Diane a chance to die in Nancy's arms.

I had put the food in the refrigerator and was turning to leave the kitchen when Kate called down the steps. I couldn't hear exactly what she said, but when I saw the shock on David and Jill's faces as they came in from the front stoop, I hurried after them up the stairs.

When I reached the master bedroom, Diane was sitting crosswise on the bed, leaning back against Nancy's chest. Nancy was murmuring, "That's right, Di, just let go," as Bach played softly in the background. I joined Nancy on the bed and placed a hand on Diane's arm. As Bill held his wife's hand, Diane's son Tim checked for a throat pulse. Everyone waited silently, looking on, looking at each other, trying to believe that what they were seeing was really happening. But was Diane still breathing? Her chest was rising and falling.

"I think that's Nancy breathing," Tim said. He checked again for a pulse. "She's gone."

Nancy continued to hold Diane in her arms, whispering, "You did it. You're home free. You're home free."

By this time, everyone in the house was in the bedroom. We seemed to have entered a kind of altered state where shock, disbelief, grief, and relief blended.

Tears flowed and ebbed and flowed again. Tessa climbed on the bed and sat next to Diane. I wasn't sure if she understood what was going on, but as she broke into sobs, it was clear she knew that her grandma was gone. Other family members crowded on the bed until it was a float of love and grief.

After several minutes, I eased myself away from Nancy's side and slid off the bed, letting others move into my spot. The grouping reminded me of a nativity scene, with friends and family gathered to mark a momentous occasion, but instead of welcoming a newborn, it was to see an old soul depart.

As the minutes passed, my mind began to wander. Where was Diane? Was her spirit still in the room?

I thought about people who have had near-death experiences. Most of them say they rose up and looked back down at their body and at the people tending to it. I wondered if Diane's spirit were looking down on us at that very moment. Would she be elated that she was finally free? Sad to see us crying? Curious about what we would do with her body?

I looked up and greeted her silently: Hi Diane! You did it!

As I gazed at the white, textured ceiling directly above Diane's body, I became aware of something transpiring. The ceiling looked solid, yet it wasn't. There was a passageway a little smaller than a manhole, some sort of portal.

I was transfixed and stared at it for a minute or two. After a while, I looked around the room, wondering if anybody else had seen the portal. But everyone was intent upon the death bed, silent or softly crying. I wanted to blurt out, "Does anyone see what's happening above the bed?" But the words wouldn't come. To speak aloud seemed not only disrespectful, but also an intrusion into each person's private experience of grief.

And what if no one else saw what I was seeing? I could hardly believe it myself. I was a businesswoman, the vice president of the company I had started fifteen years earlier, a bottom-line type of person geared to facts and figures. A hole in the ceiling? People would think I was not only disrespectful, but nuts. I kept silent, but continued to look upward.

On the other side of this portal, three beings were propped on their elbows around the opening, looking down on the scene. Only their heads appeared, and occasionally their necks, as they seemed to lean in for a closer look at times. They all had definite, but ethereal form—they were male, completely bald, wrinkle-free, but ancient.

The three stayed in their positions, equidistant from each other, but seemed to shift occasionally on their resting arms. They exuded utter peace and infinite patience. They gazed down as if looking into a well, waiting for a friend to climb up. They didn't extend a hand or cross the threshold of the open portal. They only waited. They made no sound. All of their attention was focused on Diane.

I wondered if one of these spirits was Diane's deceased father, Mr. Jansen, my eighth-grade geography teacher. But none of them resembled him and besides, these beings seemed incredibly old.

I longed for Nancy to join me so I could show her what I was seeing. Once, when someone stood up from the bed, I claimed a spot next to Nancy. I asked her if she wanted to stay in that position, hoping she wanted relief. But she was fine. She seemed to be in an altered state, and I realized she couldn't yet leave Diane. I looked up to the ceiling from the bed. The portal was still there with the three beings. I could not sense anything beyond them.

Again I stood back from the bed. I continued to observe Diane's body in Nancy's arms and the portal directly above them. I was experiencing something I'd never seen before—a person's death—and something I didn't know could happen—the other world opening to receive a spirit.

As I continued to watch the portal, I recalled a book I had read a couple of years earlier written by two Mayan scholars.[23] The book described sacred rituals that the Mayans believed dissolved the veil between this world and the next and enabled them to commune with their ancestors in the Otherworld. I suddenly realized that the portal before me must be what the Mayans were able to summon through ritual. It was their door to the spirit world.

The revelation staggered me. I was glimpsing a whole different plane of existence, a place of deep, cosmic wisdom. I felt in my bones that ancient people—the Mayans, Greeks, Egyptians—knew of this passageway and touched it in their sacred ceremonies.

I'm not sure how long the portal stayed open. Time was not flowing at its normal pace. If I had to guess, I'd say about twenty minutes. During that time, people moved around the room, some left to make calls, others joined the gathering. Eventually the portal started to fade.

I left the room when Diane's body was to be washed. As I descended the steps, I hung onto the railing, my knees wobbly. Downstairs, I sat alone in the living room, shaken to the core. I couldn't separate the emotional impact of Diane's death and the spiritual impact of the portal. They were the two sacred threads of my experience with Diane's transition, irrevocably entwined.

When I returned to the master bedroom about an hour later after the washing of the body, the portal was gone.

~

[23] Linda Schele and David Freidel, *A Forest of Kings: The Untold Story of the Ancient Maya*. New York: Quill, William Morrow, 1990.

Later that day as I mulled over the entire experience of Diane's death and the portal, a few thoughts came to me. First, that my high school English teacher was wrong. He would say on occasion, "We are born alone and we die alone." As a teenager I accepted such existential angst, but as an adult, I came to believe the first part was nonsense. Born alone! Excuse me, where is the mother in all of this? When we slip through the birth canal, it's a joint effort. A birthing baby is literally surrounded by her mother! And except in rare cases, there are ready hands waiting to catch the newborn, to lift her to a new place on earth, to tend to her immediate needs, and to place her in her mother's arms, where she can be comforted in this new world.

But now, after witnessing the death of Diane, I know we do not die alone either. Even if our passing is on a solo trip in the Amazon or up the snowy sides of Mount Everest, when the time comes, others will be gathered at the end of a different type of birth canal to enfold us and welcome us to a new home. *We are not alone.*

I thought also about death being a process, just as birth is. Diane said in her last days, "I don't know how to die." She was willing to let go, but she didn't know how. Just as her baby self knew how to slide down the birth canal, however, Diane's body knew how to handle the departure of her spirit into the ethereal passageway. Ultimately she didn't need to do a thing, except to find a way to let go. The process happened in its own time, in its own way.

Shortly after Diane's death, I read in the book, *Graceful Exits: How Great Beings Die*, that Buddhists like to die sitting up so that their spirit can more easily emerge from their seventh chakra, through the crown. This is exactly the position that Diane chose. She may not have known why, but her body and spirit guided her.

I have learned that my experience with the portal is not unique. Others have sensed the presence of a passageway at the time of death. I know now that such a doorway exists and that a gentle, loving reception is ready for all of us when our moment is at hand.

— CHAPTER FIFTEEN —

The Gift of Lavender

BECKY

In the late afternoon on the Saturday that Diane died, I was driving back to Minneapolis. Nancy was on her way to the crematorium and would stay in Mankato through Tuesday for the Life Celebration. Meanwhile, I was going home alone to get clothes for us and would return Monday for the evening wake.

During the ninety-minute drive, the events of the day played out in my head. I kept thinking of Diane dying in Nancy's arms, the family gathering in the bedroom, and my experience of seeing the portal above the bed. I still felt shaky and teary and a little bit in shock. Diane's death had happened so suddenly that it hardly seemed real.

One aspect of the day brought up self-doubts—had I been right to leave during the washing of Diane's body? When Bill had asked that only intimate female friends or family members help him wash Diane, many people disengaged themselves and went downstairs. I looked at those who were left: Diane's sister, her daughters-in-law, her only granddaughter, her dearest friends, Nancy, and Bill.

"I don't come close to the intimacy level of these people," I had said to myself. "I'd better leave."

As I drove home, I wavered between ruing and accepting that choice. I thought of the special bond formed among those who had bathed Diane's body with water infused with essential oil of lavender. It was a ritual that females have done for ages. I had never participated in this sacred rite, and I knew that I would probably never have the opportunity again.

But, I scolded myself, the ritual wasn't performed for my benefit, to give me the experience! It was done to care for and honor Diane. My petty personal desires had no place in that event.

Although I had known her for eight years, Diane and I had never been close. We had never had a serious one-on-one talk—all my conversations with her had taken place with Nancy present. I enjoyed Diane's company, laughed at her stories, and marveled at her perceptive analysis of situations, but we had never established a deep heart connection. I told myself I was right to have left the room. It would have been an intrusion on Diane's privacy. As on my drive down to Mankato in the morning when I was running late, I once again needed to trust the process.

By the time I reached the outer ring of suburbs, I was telling myself that there was no right or wrong in this situation. I had responded as I needed to at that moment and obviously I felt more compelled to leave the room than to stay. But no matter how many times I tried to trust the process, I felt torn.

When I arrived home, I unlocked the back door and stepped into the hallway at the top of the basement stairs. The most intense smell of lavender I have ever experienced hit me. It flooded the whole area.

"Diane," I exclaimed, immediately sensing the source.

I stayed on the landing for about fifteen seconds breathing in the heavy scent. I could feel Diane's presence, and I sensed her gleeful exhilaration in being without physical limitation, to be anywhere she wanted to be.

But I couldn't believe it.

Thinking that I must be mistaken—that a bottle of essential oil had broken in the basement—I ran down the steps. Everything was in place and there was absolutely no fragrance in the air. (I realized later that Nancy and I didn't even own any lavender oil.) I hurried back up to the landing by the back door where I had first experienced the piercing smell of fresh lavender. The fragrance was totally gone. There was not even a hint of it in the air.

Diane always had a remarkable ability to find perfect gifts for people. I believe that she gave me a present that day—a personal experience with lavender because I had missed the washing of her body. I felt incredibly honored that Diane would ping me with a little heart connection.

Lavender is now one of my favorite scents. We keep lavender hand soap at all of our sinks. Every time I smell it, I think of Diane and her special gift.

— CHAPTER SIXTEEN —

Two Visits and a Request

Andy Lassen and Diane were classmates at St. Olaf College in Northfield, Minnesota. An architect, Andy lives in Los Angeles, where he works as a consultant specializing in bringing older buildings up to code and combining historic preservation with accessibility for the disabled.

Even though Andy lived half a continent from Diane and Bill, the three of them stayed in touch. He saw them at least once a year when he participated in the Twin Cities marathon in the wheelchair division. He visited Diane shortly before she died. They both knew it was the last time they would ever see each other.

"Diane, this is very difficult," Andy told her. "I do not want you to leave."

She waited quietly, her hand in his.

"But I know you have to," he continued. "So go when you need to."

She squeezed his hand. "Thank you, Andy."

It was what she needed to hear from him . . . a process, he felt, of releasing and being released by the people she loved.

When Andy received the call that Diane had died, he tried to get a plane ticket and reserve a rental car with hand controls. But there was no specially equipped car available in the Twin Cities on such short notice. Not wanting to impose on the family to transport him and his wheelchair everywhere, he resigned himself to not traveling to Mankato for her funeral.

On the night of the wake, however, Diane visited him. Andy was in bed, reading as usual, before he went to sleep. He was sitting against the headboard, an architectural book propped up on the pillow in his lap. The reading lamp was on, and through the open bedroom window, he could see the skyline of downtown Los Angeles.

Suddenly Diane appeared in front of the window. She was less solid than a living person—a semi-transparent presence. Andy could see the city lights through her. Diane looked much as she did the last time he had visited, but her vibrant colors were pale, her body dim. Her eyes were still golden, which, Andy realized with surprise, only added to her beauty now.

She stood silently before him, conveying a sense of extraordinary serenity. She wordlessly communicated to him: *Andy, everything's fine. I haven't totally transcended yet, but I'm comfortable. I'm without pain. I'm on this path, and everything is fine.*

The serenity that permeated Diane's spirit was familiar to Andy. He had had two near-death experiences many years earlier, and both times he had felt that same profound peace.

Then Diane spoke to him. He heard her rich, warm voice clearly.

"Andy, stay close to Bill. He is going to need you."

He felt thrilled to be hearing Diane's voice, her intonation, her way of saying his name.

Then the image became cloudy, and she faded away.

Although Andy felt immensely consoled by Diane's appearance, he was troubled by the urgency in her message. Her request made no sense to Andy. Bill was one of the healthiest, most competent people he had ever met. He couldn't imagine Bill needing him for one second.

Two nights later, as he was reading in bed, it happened again.

There was Diane, semi-transparent, standing immobile in front of his bedroom window, again radiating serenity.

"Stay close to Bill," she repeated. "He is going to need you."

More quickly this time, she faded away and disappeared.

For weeks afterwards, although Andy still didn't understand her message, he felt deeply comforted and honored that Diane had chosen to visit him, not once, but twice. Her serene appearances assuaged his disappointment at having had to miss the final good-byes of her memorial service.

In the years since then, Andy has maintained his friendship with Bill. When he runs in the annual Twin Cities Marathon, Bill is there to cheer him on. The next day, they make time for a good talk and a long walk around one of the lakes in Minneapolis.

Neither Andy nor Bill knows what to make of Diane's message. Since they haven't been able to figure it out, they are letting the future reveal itself, both of them grateful to have known and loved this remarkable woman.

— CHAPTER SEVENTEEN —

The Dreams

As part of her nursing program at Mankato State University, Sue Towey chose to do a clinical psychiatric rotation. Her supervisor was Diane. After graduating in 1975, Sue had several community nursing and mental health jobs. In 1980, she started working at the Mankato Psychiatric Clinic, where Diane worked. During the years she and Diane were at the clinic, they became close friends. They co-facilitated several therapy groups, including a weekly women's psychotherapy group that lasted for almost ten years.

Outside the clinic, they played tennis, walked, biked, and cross-country skied together. They also traveled to Mental Health and Advanced Practice Nursing professional conferences. Their psychotherapy practices helped them get to know each other in unusually intimate ways. After Sue moved to Minneapolis in 1990, they saw each other less, but their ties of nursing, psychotherapy, and deep friendship remained strong.

Sue's first dream about Diane took place six months after her death. In the dream, Sue and Diane were running through a grassy field toward each other. When they met, they jumped up and down with joy. They stood in the sunshine, laughing at the absurd but wonderful experience of being together again even though Diane was dead.

They shared news about their lives and their children. Diane told Sue about her beloved granddaughter Tessa. They talked freely, companionably, and deeply, as they had always talked. The light of the sun enveloped them, filling Sue with joy and love. Time seemed eternal, as though their meeting would last forever.

When she woke, Sue realized that Diane had blessed her with a full body experience. She felt suffused with a peaceful joy, a feeling that stayed with her for days.

Sue recognized this sensation from her near-death experience twenty-five years earlier. She had been brutally assaulted and left for dead. Despite her critical injuries, Sue was flooded by what she calls "an experience of eternal love, peace, and joy." Diane had been very interested in Sue's mystical experience at that time, and, over the years, they had examined many aspects of it together.

After she recovered, Sue continued her career as a psychiatric nurse with a new passion for transformational work. She dedicated herself to helping patients gain access to the spiritual reserves deep within themselves. She also began giving nonviolence workshops through the Mankato Psychiatric Clinic and speaking at Mankato's Center Against Domestic Abuse.

Sue's second dream occurred a year after Diane died. In this dream, in another outdoor setting, Bill was with Diane. After greeting the couple, Sue walked toward a grassy knoll, where Diane joined her. Diane was about fifteen years younger than when she died.

Sue told Diane about her reaction to the previous dream, ending with the observation, "You really are alive, even though we know you're dead." Again they laughed at the absurdity. Diane said, "I know I'm dead, but I wanted to catch up. And actually, I'm not really dead, you know. I will always be alive."

They chatted for a while, again about their families. When they tried to place incidents in a time frame, they used Diane's death as the marker. "That happened before you died, right?" or "That must have been after I died."

At the end of the conversation, Diane gave Sue a long hug. She could feel Diane's body as warm and solid as if she were alive.

These two dreams have remained vivid. They have helped Sue continue her connection of spirit with Diane and to be at peace with the loss of her dearest friend.

— CHAPTER EIGHTEEN —

A Different Frequency

Diane had a talent for making children feel like real people. She would get down on their level and look them in the eye when speaking. She knew how to be with them, and she took them seriously.

Part of Diane's job at the Mankato Psychiatric Clinic was facilitating a therapeutic activity group for children. She brought her remarkable understanding of children as well as her professional skills to that group. She also brought creativity and the ability to think outside the box.

Diane and Bill had been close friends with Mary and Chuck Lofy since the early 1970s, and their seven children often played together. Annmarie Lofy Rubin recalls that when her two brothers ran off to play with the four Manahan boys, she would stay with Diane, who seemed to know exactly what she needed. Diane would have paper dolls and the makings of a tea party ready for the little girl.

When Annmarie was twelve years old, Diane asked her to be a "co-therapist" for her children's group at the clinic. Diane envisioned a child facilitator helping other children feel more comfortable and open. She also knew that Annmarie could model appropriate behavior that would be helpful to the group process. This was unprecedented, indeed heretical, for therapy practice in the 1980s, but Diane trained Annmarie and implemented her plan. The results were excellent, and Annmarie worked with Diane for two years, during which time they developed a deep friendship. Years later, Diane published an article about the experience.[24]

The two stayed close over the years, even after Annmarie graduated, attended the University of Wisconsin in Madison, and later moved to Ann Arbor, Michigan. When Diane's cancer reappeared, they started writing long thoughtful letters to each other. Two months before Diane died, Annmarie brought her new baby to Mankato so Diane could meet her and bless her.

Throughout this time, Annmarie struggled to come to terms with Diane's terminal cancer. She mourned the imminent loss of Diane's friendship, humor, and wisdom. For as long as she could remember, she had been terribly afraid of death, and now she felt fearful about what would happen to Diane after her death.

On Labor Day weekend, six weeks after Diane's death, Annmarie had a sleep-state experience that was more than a dream. She was washing her hands in a large outdoor room covered with lush green vines, their tendrils entwined on supports along the sides and overhead to form verdant walls and a ceiling. In front of her was a huge bay mirror. Suddenly Diane appeared in the mirror wearing one of her exquisite, vividly-colored outfits.

Annmarie caught her breath, unable to take her eyes off the mirror. Diane smiled warmly at her. She was afraid to turn, fearful that Diane would disappear. But she finally turned to face her beloved friend.

"Diane, I can't believe you're here!" Annmarie cried. "I can't believe I'm seeing you."

"You mean because I'm dead?" Diane said in her typical blunt manner.

"What are you doing here? You're so alive, so vibrant!"

---

[24] "Abbie – A Child Group Co-Leader," *Beginnings*, Vol. 10, No. 2, February 1990.

Diane said, "I've been given a rare opportunity to come back and take care of some unfinished business."

Annmarie wondered how Diane, of all people, could have unfinished business. She had been so thorough in her professional and personal life. Her dying process had been unusually intentional, down to the impeccably-planned life celebration.

She broke out of her thoughts. "What's it like?"

"Do you mean, what is death like?"

Suddenly the scene changed. They were surrounded by dense fog. Annmarie couldn't see anything except a vague image of Diane. But she could hear Diane's warm, rich pre-cancer voice.

"Well, Annmarie, I can't really tell you because I haven't totally crossed over yet. If I had, I wouldn't be able to be here talking to you. But what I want you to know is that dying is just like moving to a different frequency. You don't have to be afraid. It's just like tuning to a different radio frequency."

A deep sense of peace surrounded and permeated Annmarie.

Then the scene changed again and Annmarie thought, oh no, my time with her is over.

She found herself in another verdant outdoor room. Beautiful vines and flowers formed a canopy, like a huge *chupa* at a Jewish wedding. Diane was sitting in the grass under the canopy, talking to her friend Susie Symons.

As she watched the two women deep in conversation, Annmarie realized that Diane's unfinished business didn't have to do with Diane's issues. She had returned to help those who needed her.

When she awoke, Annmarie felt as though she had really been with Diane. She called Bill and told him about her dream, and she shared it with her parents. As she did so, she realized that her attitude toward death had changed. She no longer felt panic when she thought about dying. Diane's words had dissolved her fear, and in its place was a calm acceptance.

— CHAPTER NINETEEN —

A Second Chance

In Annmarie Rubin's sleep-state experience, Diane was talking with Susie Symons. A year later, close to Labor Day weekend, Susie herself had an important communication from Diane.

Susie and Diane had been friends for thirty years. Even after Susie left Mankato for Michigan in 1980, she and Diane communicated regularly, and the two couples spent time together every year. After Diane's cancer returned, Susie visited as often as possible, and their correspondence deepened. A few weeks before her death, Diane asked Susie to read one of her favorite letters at the Life Celebration.[25]

When Diane died, Susie canceled all appointments with her psychotherapy clients, took the next flight to Minneapolis and spent several days in Mankato, grieving with Diane's family and other friends. She deeply regretted not being with Diane during her very last days and missing the moment of her death. During the next year, her grief remained intense.

In July 2002, Susie's eighty-six-year-old mother, to whom she

[25] See "Appendix E: Eulogy from Susie Symons."

was very close, was diagnosed with an inoperable brain tumor. Medication kept Ginnie alert for only a month, during which time Susie traveled to Massachusetts for extended periods to be with her.

Ten days before Labor Day, her mother slipped into a coma. Susie was torn. Months earlier, she had purchased airline tickets to Seattle to attend the wedding of a good friend. Shouldn't she return to Massachusetts instead? The doctors reassured her that Ginnie might linger in a coma for weeks, and wouldn't even know that Susie was there. Moreover, Ginnie's close friends were taking turns sitting beside her bed; she was being watched over. Both Susie's father, a physician, and her sister urged her to go to the wedding and do something joyful—something to alleviate the anguish of the past weeks. And besides, they said, if she didn't go, she would have to forfeit the cost of the tickets. Still, she remained conflicted about what to do.

In that state of uncertainty, Susie went to her regular therapy appointment. Her therapist used Eye Movement Desensitization and Reprocessing (EMDR), a therapy involving alternating stimulation of each hemisphere of the brain using eye movements, which helps to "process" or work through distress.

As the EMDR session began, Susie focused on her conflict about where she should travel. Soon she had a crystal-clear thought that she *knew* came from Diane. It was as if she could hear Diane's speaking in her head. "Your Mom's been your oldest and best friend since before you were born. Where else could you be right now?"

After a few moments another thought came. "You were so sad not to be with me when I died. This is your opportunity."

Then a few seconds later she heard, "I'll meet you there."

Susie was certain the source of this communication was Diane. The succinct wisdom, the choice of words, and the energy were all Diane's. And wasn't it what Diane had done so often when she was alive—provide insight at perplexing forks in the road? Susie now knew what to do.

She and John left for Massachusetts at five thirty the next morning, driving ten hours straight. When they arrived at the assisted living retirement home, Susie dashed up the stairs, eager to be with her mother again. But of course, Ginnie was unconscious—and to Susie, who'd never been with someone in a coma—totally and startlingly unresponsive.

Suspecting that EMDR might help her mother's brain, in the late afternoon Susie fitted her own headphones over her mother's ears and played an EMDR tape for twenty minutes—gentle tones, first one ear and then the other. Two hours later, Ginnie opened her magnificent blue eyes for the first time in ten days, and looked directly at Susie and John. As her daughter and son-in-law moved around the room, she tracked them with her eyes for the rest of the evening.

The next morning, when Susie and John arrived, she was not only awake, but propped up in bed! She looked directly into Susie's eyes and said softly, "I didn't think I'd still be here for this!"

Susie flew to her mother's embrace, astonished that she was "back." And for the next forty-eight hours, Ginnie was conscious much of the time, holding hands with those by her bedside, speaking occasionally—sometimes with empathy, sometimes even with humor.

On the second day of Ginnie's return to consciousness, her physician's wife brought their young daughter to say goodbye to the woman who'd been her "almost grandmother" for twelve years. She was so amazed to see Ginnie awake that she called her husband, who arrived with their teenage son. After a few minutes, the doctor motioned Susie to come outside into the atrium. He told her that over many years of being a physician, he'd come to respect how "tough" the elderly were, and that he'd seen many "rallies," when patients would find strength to hold on to life until a certain event came to pass.

"But I've never seen anything like this," he said. "This is absolutely amazing!"

Susie, John, and the others who visited were profoundly grateful for the miracle of those last precious days of consciousness with Ginnie.

On the third morning, Ginnie was in a coma again, and remained so for the whole day. With her father at Ginnie's bedside, Susie and John left for supper. As they were leaving the restaurant, the cell phone rang.

"Come as fast as you can," said the nurse.

Two minutes before they arrived at her room, Susie's mother died.

Once again Susie had missed the moment of death. But it felt acceptable this time. She had been with her mother in all the important ways, and had enjoyed those two extraordinary days of having Ginnie awake and aware.

Susie wrapped her mother in a shroud of her favorite color, lavender, which she'd sewn and embroidered with the names her mother had been called: Ginnie, Mom, G.G., and Great G.G. Still covered by this cloth, her mother's body was taken to the hearse.

Afterwards, Susie and John stayed in the empty room. They both sensed an unusual energy, an exquisitely gentle pulsating vibration, which subsided over the next one and a half hours. They sensed her mother's spirit gradually withdrawing. When the vibrations were completely gone, Susie called Diane's husband. She told Bill that her mom had died. About the experience of transition, she said simply, "I get it now."

Although she wasn't aware of Diane at her mother's bedside, Susie felt different when she left her mother's room that night. Experiencing death and the ending/beginning it marked, she felt at peace with the loss not only of her mother, but also of her beloved friend. Her grief about Diane—which had seemed unbearable for over a year—felt resolved.

Ever since this experience, Susie sometimes senses Diane's energy just behind her right shoulder, and her mother's energy behind her left. This awareness happens most often during puzzling times in psychotherapy sessions with her clients. Their presence eases the moment and provides a comforting, dependable compass.

Diane and Susie Symons
in Hawaii to visit herbalist Papa Henry
Fall 1999

Epilogue

For all of her meticulous planning, one item did not make it to Diane's to-do list: a physical marker commemorating her life on earth. Ironically, while she wanted to be remembered, she didn't care about a marker. Her family and friends, however, realized that they wanted a spot where they could "visit" her. Should it be something like a gravestone, or another type of memorial, such as a tree? Should it be in Madelia, where Diane grew up, or in Mankato, which she loved and where she lived most of her adult life?

Eventually, her family envisioned a sculpture in Sibley Park. As befit the spirit of Diane, her marker would not be a traditional gravestone in a cemetery, but rather a big natural rock, accessible to anyone, in the middle of a public park. Perhaps it could depict the wee people (leprechauns) of Ireland, a Manahan family tradition that Diane loved and which delighted children.

A week after her death, Tim and Kate started searching for the right stone. One hot afternoon, sculptor Tom Miller took the couple, their two toddlers, and Bill to a nearby limestone quarry, where after two hours of searching, they discovered a large chunk of golden Kasota stone between patches of long grass. One side had a natural platform that could be fitted with a stone slab seat, and the rest formed a block for kids to scramble around on. They had found an ideal memorial.

The artist transported the block back to his studio to fashion the stone bench. Bill, Tim, and Kate decided to forgo the leprechauns. Children playing on Diane's bench would be the real wee people.

Bill and several family members crafted the words for a memorial plaque which was attached to the stone. It reads:

IN MEMORY OF
DIANE JANSEN MANAHAN (1940–2001)
WHO LOVED SIBLEY PARK.
SHE SAW BEAUTY AND CREATIVITY
IN ALL OF LIFE AND HONORED
THE GIFTS OF EACH OF US.

The Sibley Park ground crew prepared a base for the bench, which the sculptor installed in time for the one-year anniversary celebration. The stone was positioned among the five evergreens that Diane and her closest friends had planted years before. This memorial, says her son Mike, is "the ultimate tribute. It's so much like Mom. It's exactly what she would have chosen—a local, natural, unpolished, beautiful rock."

The dedication of Diane's memorial took place on August 6th, her birthday, following the annual family reunion that had brought many relatives to Minnesota. Family members and close friends gathered around the Kasota stone in Sibley Park. We sang Happy Birthday to Diane, and each of us had a chance to speak what was in our hearts. At the end of the ceremony, Bill removed his wedding ring and gave it to his oldest grandson, Jansen Manahan. The ritual allowed Bill to move on to a new phase of his life.

After the ceremony we caravanned to the Mankato YMCA, to see the beautiful ceramic artwork that Diane had commissioned from John Glick. The next stop was the university to see Diane's Room, a nook in the school of nursing where students can relax and study. Thanks to Laura Turk and Bev Palmquist, the décor had a lovely, cozy Diane-look. A stained glass work of art, created by Catherine Bourret, wove together elements that Diane treasured:

sun, water, and earth.

Finally, we gathered at Bill and Diane's house and had a birthday party for Diane. Everyone brought what they thought was Diane's favorite food. We brought Cheez-Its, Ruth arrived with the ham loaf she had often made especially for Diane, Kate had baked banana bread, and Bill had stuffed the freezer with Häagen-Dazs coffee ice cream.

It may have been the unhealthiest meal ever served in that house, but we enjoyed Diane's treats immensely. Bill and Di knew the importance of good nutrition, as their kids could attest growing up on brown rice and vegetables. But Diane had believed in balance. "There's nothing better than fat and sugar!" she'd exclaim while popping a handful of peanut M&Ms. Indeed, one of her favorite sayings was "Everything in moderation, including moderation!"

As we ate, music from a memorial CD compiled by Jon Olseth played in the background. Jon had recorded the song he wrote for Diane in a professional studio and with Bill's help, filled the CD with love songs special to Diane and Bill. The insert contained photos of Diane and her family. Jill's pen-and-ink African women danced across the bottom margin. Bill's liner notes read:

> Diane loved music with a style that made singing or playing music with her seem like a spiritual experience. Music always held a special reverence for Diane. She sang in her high school and college choirs, played the drums in high school, sang the Messiah with a choir almost every Easter, delighted in practicing on her cello, loved singing as she played show tunes on the piano, and exhilarated in attending symphony concerts and theatrical musical productions. Diane was song, and Diane was music . . . Love songs seemed to be the very essence of who Diane was—the most loving, most listening, and most compassionate person I have ever known.

Two years after Diane's death, Bill moved to Minneapolis, and now he lives with us. The redwood box with Diane's ashes is in his bedroom. On the buffet in the living room, a spot the three of us pass dozens of times a day, we keep a framed photograph of Diane reading to their granddaughter, Tessa. The expression of mutual adoration on their faces says it all.

~

Living Consciously, Dying Gracefully: A Journey with Cancer and Beyond reveals the outcomes of the choices Diane Manahan made at every stage of her five-and-a-half-year journey with cancer as her companion. She chose to go through the experience and to die as she had lived: with balance, humor, consciousness, and grace. She nurtured relationships right up to the day she died—and beyond—making openings for everyone to have closure with her. She showed us all how to face our own mortality with dignity and truth.

We offer this book as a tribute to one of the most fully alive and authentic people we have ever known. We hope that it can provide comfort to those in pain and information to those who seek it. May it inspire us to follow Diane's philosophy as recorded in her journal: *To treat people with dignity whether I agree with them or not; to give reverence to nature and creation; to err with some grace and humor; to maintain and share my sense of fun.*

For all that Diane has been to us, shared with us, and taught us, we are grateful. We wish her joy and peace on her continuing soul journey.

Becky Bohan and Nancy Manahan
Minneapolis, Minnesota
February 2007

Diane Manahan's Kasota Stone Bench Memorial
Sibley Park, Mankato, Minnesota
Tessa Stevenson Manahan and Jansen William Manahan (upper level)
Teliz Stevenson Manahan and Owen Turpin Manahan (lower level)
August 2002

Diane's husband Bill and sons Mike, Topher, David, and Tim
Manahan Family Reunion
Cedar Valley Resort, Whalen, Minnesota
August 2005

— GUIDEBOOK —

Lessons from Diane on Dealing with a Serious Illness or Death

Guidebook Contents

Introduction

The material in this guidebook is compiled from 1) the chapters of *Living Consciously, Dying Gracefully: A Journey with Cancer and Beyond;* 2) data from Bill and Diane Manahan's files not included in the body of this book; 3) our observations about Diane and her family's handling of her illness and death; and 4) information from other sources. The easy-to-read format can be used as a checklist or as talking points for discussions.

The suggestions reflect Diane's personal attitudes and her individual journey. They are not meant to be prescriptive or comprehensive. Take what you like, and explore other resources. See "Recommended Resources" at the end of this book for a few additional ideas.

If You Are Diagnosed with a Serious Illness

~ Consider the mystery of your situation. If you don't want to delve deep and try to figure out the "cause" or "meaning" of your illness, you don't have to.

~ Fend off guilt that well-meaning friends may prompt when they say, "Why do you think you got this?" Illness can be simply a physical process.

~ Don't be rushed into making decisions. Take the time needed to inform yourself. The more information you have, the better.

› Consult with doctors. What have they done for others in a situation similar to yours? What were the results? Write down your questions beforehand. Invite someone who can take notes and debrief with you afterwards. It's helpful if that person is knowledgeable about medicine.

› If possible, get a second opinion. Overwhelmed doctors may dislike your request for another opinion, but your physician is your partner in your health care journey. You are in charge and—in one form or another—you are paying for your care.

› Use libraries and reliable Internet sources to gather information about your illness and treatment options.

› Check with local and national organizations that can supply you with current information.

› Research complementary care appropriate for your illness. Consult with holistic practitioners and ask what they can do for you. What have they done for others in a situation similar to yours? What were the results? Take someone with you, as you would for a doctor's appointment.

› Find a "coach"—someone who can help you sift through all the information. It can be a partner, a friend, or a volunteer at a support organization.

If You Are Going through Treatment

~ Determine your approach to your illness and let it be a guidepost. If you think of it as war, go to battle. If you think of it as a nonviolent intervention to help an uninvited guest to depart, build your care plan in terms of peaceful images and actions.

~ Expect to have a mix of feelings. Find emotional support that works for you, from trusted friends and family members, support groups, counseling, and prayer and healing circles.

~ Find what nourishes your soul—being in nature, praying, laughing with friends, playing music, shopping, reading spiritual books—and do those things as much as possible.

~ Share your experience with family members and friends who are capable of being supportive. Take loved ones with you to appointments and treatments.

~ If you do not want to deal with day-to-day chores, don't. Hire help or ask friends for help. Designate a care coordinator—someone who can organize friends and family to shop, cook meals, do chores, walk the dog, or distract and entertain you.

~ Nourish a positive attitude, but let all your feelings have opportunities for safe expression.

~ Practice relaxation and visualization.

~ Treasure healing moments. Be grateful for whatever is precious in your life.

If You Are Facilitating a Support Group

~ If you are not a trained facilitator, get training in facilitation and group dynamics. It will help you create a safe space, make sure that everyone gets the time needed to share their concerns, and maintain the distinction between a support group and a therapy session.

~ Choose the space carefully. It should be private, wheelchair accessible, well-located, and an appropriate size.

~ Eight or so members is an optimal size. The group should have a clear understanding of attendance requirements and the length of the series of meetings.

~ Charging a minimal amount for the sessions can help attendance and relieve costs to the sponsoring organization.

~ Don't have any preconceived notions about what type of interactions should occur within the group.

~ Presenting information isn't nearly as important as sharing stories and gleaning information through the group members' own experiences.

~ Having tea available is a nurturing touch.

~ Members like checking in and having each others' phone numbers and addresses.

~ Encourage light-hearted playfulness. Members will welcome opportunities to laugh.

~ Be aware that members may be very affected when someone in the group has a recurrence or dies.

~ Be aware of your own issues and triggers. Pass facilitation to someone else when necessary.

~ Make sure everyone agrees to confidentiality. Nothing said in a group should be discussed with nonmembers.

If You Are Terminally Ill

~ Ask for what you need, whether it is pain relief, quiet alone-time, a visit, a wish.

~ Determine what you want regarding discussing your terminal condition. If you want to talk to others about it, tell them. If you don't want to talk about it, ask them not to bring up the subject.

~ Check out hospice in your area. Hospice offers extremely helpful services to the terminally ill and their families, and support for those who wish to die at home including in-home comfort care. Hospice workers can counsel family members, provide pain medication, facilitate discussions of end-of-life choices, and help in a crisis.[26]

~ Focus on what has the most truth and meaning for you, whether that be family, friends, home, animals, paid or volunteer work, organizations, community, special projects, or your creativity.

~ Decide how you would like your last years/months to be. If you want to be as healthy and active as possible, you may want to forego aggressive medical treatments that could leave you exhausted, miserable, and financially depleted.

~ Eat what you like, what nourishes you, and what gives you pleasure.

~ Make a record of your life. It will help you see your accomplishments, identify things you may yet want to do, and leave a history for your loved ones.

~ Find ways to complete any unfinished business, such as saying "I'm sorry," "Thank you," "I love you," or "I forgive you" to

---

[26] Visit the National Hospice and Palliative Care Organization website for more information: www.nhpco.org.

whoever needs those messages from you. Say good-bye to the people who matter. Make time for others to say good-bye to you.

~ Honor your path and do not feel the need to conform to other people's expectations. Each person experiences dying in his or her own way.

~ Give yourself permission to have days when you are not up to doing any of the above.

If You Are Planning Your End-of-Life Experience

Consider how you would like to die and discuss it with your partner and/or caregivers. Questions to ask yourself include:

~ Do you want to die at home? In a hospice facility? In a hospital? Make back-up plans so your caregivers have options in case your first choice isn't possible.

~ To what extent do you want to be in charge of your pain medication?

~ What types of medical tests do you want/not want performed on you?

~ If your heart stops, do you want to be resuscitated? If not, you need a Do Not Resuscitate order as well as a Living Will. If you are in a care facility, a "Do Not Resuscitate" sign should be in your charts and posted on your door.

~ Whom do you want with you when you die?

~ What will provide you with comfort on your deathbed? Do you want music playing? Ask for whatever you want. Don't be afraid to change your mind.

Making Plans for After You Die

Think about what you want to happen after you die and discuss it with your family and/or caregivers. Questions to ask yourself include:

~ When you die, how do you want your body handled? Do you want to be washed and dressed by those close to you? If yes, determine how that is to be done. Do you prefer professionals to handle your body?

~ Do you want/not want to be embalmed? Cremated? Do you want a casket? An urn?

~ If finances are an issue, research costs of each service from a mortuary. There is a wide range. If you have specified a low-cost service, your loved ones will not feel they are being "cheap."

~ Do you want a viewing of your body? If so, where do you want it viewed? What clothing do you want to wear?

~ Make sure your loved ones have the legal powers to carry out your wishes.

~ Find a mortician who will follow your directions.

~ Determine what kind of service, memorial, or celebration you want. Remember, this is a time to honor your life. Don't be shy.

~ When death comes, whom do you want notified? Where are their telephone numbers or e-mail addresses?

~ What do you want in your obituary? Do you want to write the basic text yourself or have someone else write it?

~ What type of legacy do you want to leave? Identify any organizations that you wish to receive money.

~ Do you want to create a remembrance for your loved ones? It can be as simple as giving away photos or writing a card. It can be as artful as making a scrapbook full of pictures and descriptions of your life's highlights. It could be a personal video or a site on the Internet.

~ Do you want to make presents of some of your belongings while you are still alive?

~ Get your paperwork in order. Get all your insurance and legal documents in one folder.[27] Do you want to destroy journals or pass them on to someone?

~ Do you have unfinished projects you can pass on or train someone to finish?

~ Develop your own ways to be at peace with the dying process. You will know when the time is right to leave, just as you knew when the time was right to be born.

---

[27] See "Appendix C: Resolve to Organize by Vanda Manahan, Ph.D." for guidelines.

Ideas for the Caregivers of a Person Who is Dying

~ Learn about the common stages of dying. Many people follow a predictable pattern in the weeks, days and hours leading up to their death. Knowing about these stages can help you feel more comfortable and more able to comfort your loved one.[28]

~ For some, death is a process of movement during which there can be a wavering between this world and the next. Don't be alarmed if your loved one talks about experiences or people you don't see.

~ Let the dying process happen in the way your loved one wants. You are there to support her or him. Make the setting as comfortable, respectful, and loving as possible.

~ Organize a phone tree or e-mail list, or designate one person to pass on updates.

~ If the death is at home, know whom to contact once your loved one dies, including:

› The physician or other official who can sign the death certificate. (Rules vary by states.)

› The mortician, if one is involved.

› Loved ones who will want to partake in any rituals or ceremonies or need to say their last good-bye.

› People responsible for organizing the funeral, memorial service, or life celebration.

---

[28] Recommended pamphlet: *Gone from My Sight* by Barbara Karnes, RN (BK Books, Inc., second edition 2005).

Helping Someone Who Is Having a Seizure

If you have never seen a seizure, it can be an alarming experience. Normally, a person having a seizure requires little assistance other than caring support and observation. Once started, seizures cannot be stopped abruptly. Most seizures will end naturally. Generally, seizures are not painful and the person does not have any memory of them.[29]

Here are a few tips:

~ Clear the area of sharp objects or anything else that could be dangerous. Protect the person's head from being bumped.

~ If possible, help the person lie on his or her side to keep the airway open.

~ Do not put anything in the person's mouth.

~ Do not attempt to restrain a person's arms or legs during a seizure.

~ Most seizures last several minutes. Try not to panic if it goes on longer than you expect.

~ After a seizure, the person may be confused. This is normal. Tell the person where she or he is and what happened. Allow time to rest and recover.

---

[29] Adapted from *A Primer of Brain Tumors: Patient's Reference Manual*, 8th Edition, 2004, p. 54. Used with permission of the American Brain Tumor Association.

Caring for the Body

~ Respect the wishes of your loved one when it comes to the handling of the body.

~ If they requested washing and dressing of their body, have at hand all the materials you will need:

› A towel or sheet to slip under the body

› A wash basin, soap, a soothing essential oil such as lavender, washcloths, and towels

› A way to collect any urine in the bladder (a catheter, towel, or pad)

› A way to prevent bowel fluid from leaking out (a soft cloth or wad of cotton)

~ Be aware of the time limits and state regulations for having a body in your home. Temperature can affect the body. If necessary, use dry ice to keep the body cool and reduce unpleasant odors.[30]

---

[30] See sources of information listed in "Recommended Resources."

Holding a Visitation or Vigil

~ Determine the place and hours of the visitation/vigil.

~ Prepare a list of people to contact, along with their phone numbers. If you are going through a mortuary, the mortician can place an announcement in the paper.

~ Determine beforehand who will make phone calls or send e-mails letting people know.

~ If the visitation/vigil will be in your home, make the setting for the body as simple, comfortable, and beautiful as possible. Choose the chairs, music, photos, flowers and/or candles carefully.

~ If the visitation/vigil will be in a funeral home or chapel, follow the wishes of your loved one regarding an open or closed casket and other displays.

Accompanying the Body to a Crematorium

~ Make arrangements beforehand with the mortician so that once your loved one dies, you will know what you can legally do. Know the procedures to follow.

~ If you want to have someone present with the body at all times, designate beforehand who those people will be and how the transportation will be arranged.

~ Be prepared for a wait of some hours while the body is being cremated.

~ If you would like to see the skeletal remains before they are pulverized, ask to do so.

~ Accompanying the body of a loved one through its final stages can be a way to honor the person. It can also be a way to let go of your loved one as you experience the finality of his or her physical transformation.

Holding a Wake

Traditionally, a wake is held on one of the evenings shortly after a death but before the memorial service or funeral. A wake may involve simply watching over the body, whether it is in a casket or ashes in an urn, or it may involve activities. Here are some ideas for holding a wake:

~ Follow the wishes of your loved one. If she or he did not communicate any specific desires, determine what would be most appropriate. Will the wake involve close friends and family or a wider circle?

~ Decide who will lead the wake, invite people to share, and bring the event to a close.

~ Set out candles and pictures of your loved one. Choose any music you want to be playing in the background.

~ Before they come, invite people to prepare to share poems, stories, and memories of the deceased. Contributions will be richer if some thought is put into them ahead of time.

~ Decide what food and drink to serve. It can be a nice touch to have some of your loved one's favorite foods available.

Holding a Memorial Service/Life Celebration

~ This is the final public good-bye. Set an appropriate tone, and, as much as possible, follow the wishes of your loved one.

~ Have a plan in place. There are so many details that the more prepared you are, the better. A written plan can serve as a checklist. Some of the items to consider:

› Where will the celebration take place? If it is a public place, who will get the permits? Will you need a microphone and loudspeakers? If so, where do you rent them and how do you hook them up?

› Do you want a display of pictures, a video, or computer slide presentation? Who will assemble pictures or arrange for the equipment?

› Is childcare needed? Who will be in charge of it?

› Who should lead the ceremony? Who should participate in the ceremony? What do you want them to do?

› Do you want poems or special passages to be read? Who will be the readers? Do you want an open microphone for people to share their thoughts?

› What music will be playing before, during, and after the service? If you have live music, who will be the performers?

› What rituals would you like performed?

› What do you want the program to say? Who will design, write, and print the program?

› Who will be the pall-bearers/life-bearers?

› Who will provide the refreshments? What kind should they be?

› What kind of decorations and flowers do you want?

› How do you want the remains represented at the ceremony?

› Will the ceremony involve going to the cemetery? Releasing ashes?

~ Accept offers of help. Delegate. Delegate. Delegate.

— APPENDICES —

Diane and Bill at home, June 2001
One month before Diane's death

Appendix A
A Summary of Healing Philosophies

by Bill Manahan, M.D.

1. Allopathic Medicine

This system of medical practice combats disease by treatments that produce effects different from those produced by the disease treated. An allopath would treat an inflammation or infection with an anti-inflammatory (aspirin) or anti-infective (penicillin). The cause of most disease is believed to be physical. Treatment relies on surgery, radiation, and pharmaceuticals.

2. Biomolecular Medicine

This is also called Nutritional, Orthomolecular, or Functional Medicine. It employs assessment and early intervention to improve physiological, emotional/cognitive, and physical function. It uses applied nutritional science through a spectrum of therapeutic biological modifiers such as dietary nutrients and supplements, phytochemicals, and nutrient medicinal foods.

3. Botanical Medicine

This is the philosophy of using plant material as medicinal agents to heal disease and prevent illness. Approximately 25% of pharmaceutical prescriptions contain ingredients isolated from plants.

4. Environmental Medicine

This medical philosophy (formerly called Clinical Ecology) deals with environmental hazards including chemicals, ionizing radiation, air pollution, sensitizing substances, social and work settings, and communicable disease. Environmental illness is usually a polysymptomatic, multisystem chronic disorder manifested by adverse reactions to environmental excitants (foods, inhalants, chemicals) as they are modified by individual susceptibility. In other words, there are environmental substances (excitants) in our air, water, food, drugs, and habitat, and we all react to them biochemically in a uniquely individual manner. The manner in which a certain percentage of people react causes illness. Environmental medicine physicians also frequently work with patients having chronic fatigue syndrome, systemic candidiasis, and ordinary allergies. As opposed to ordinary allergies, environmental illness is a response to toxins in the environment through pathways not necessarily mediated by the immune system. Environmental illness is a toxic but not always immunological reaction to foreign substances.

5. Ethnomedicine

This area refers to beliefs and medical practices of traditional cultural groups, including those whose knowledge and practices have been transmitted orally for centuries.

AYURVEDIC MEDICINE is a branch of traditional Indian Medicine. *Ayurvedic* is from Sanskrit: *ayus* means life and *veda* means knowledge or science. It is translated as "the science of life." Disease is seen as an imbalance in the life force (*prana*), or it may be karmically preordained. Central to Ayurvedic diagnosis and treatment is the principle of biologic individuality. It sees the individual characteristics of each person as the primary factor in the etiology of disease and emphasizes the mental and emotional causes of imbalances. Three irreducible principles (called *doshas*) regulate the different functions of mind and body. They are Vata, Pitta and Kapha. The proportion in each person determines the psychophysiological type of that person. Its yoga and meditation practices are aspects of Ayurveda familiar to many people.

NATIVE AMERICAN MEDICINE and spirituality together form the basis of healing and health. Everyone is connected to and has some sort of direct relationship with the Creator. It involves a respect for all of God's creations including plants, animals, and humans. Earth, air, fire and water are important energies involved with Native American medicine and ceremonies. Disease is caused by some disharmony in the cosmic order as well as by hexing, breaking a taboo, fright or soul loss.

TRADITIONAL CHINESE MEDICINE is an ancient method of health care that combines the use of medicinal herbs, acupuncture, changes in diet, massage, and therapeutic exercise. TCM looks for underlying causes of imbalances and patterns of disharmony in the body, and it views each patient as unique. A diagnosis might include describing the body in terms of the elements—wind, heat, cold, dryness, dampness. Yin is used to refer to the tissue of the organ and yang refers to its activity. TCM works with qi, the life force that is all-inclusive of the many types of energy within the body and flows through the body in pathways called meridians. For diagnosis, the TCM practitioner takes a good history and performs at least five methods of investigation: inspection of the pulses, complexion, general demeanor, body language, and tongue.

6. Fitness/Exercise Medicine

This philosophy employs the use of aerobic and anaerobic methods to help an individual be well adapted to his or her environment and able to respond to its changing demands. Aerobic exercise is an activity that increases the heart and respiratory rate so extra oxygen is needed. Anaerobic exercises are those in which increased oxygen is not needed. These include stretching, muscle toning, muscle building, and activities designed to improve balance, flexibility, agility, and coordination.

7. *Energy Medicine*

This is an area of medical practice that involves subtle or very low intensity nonmaterial stimuli. Examples are homeopathy, acupuncture, electromagnetic therapies, Reiki, therapeutic touch, Jin Shin Jyutsu, light and color techniques, Qigong, and Tai Chi.

HOMEOPATHY is a natural pharmaceutical science that uses micro doses of substances to stimulate the immune defense system of one's body. Substances from the mineral, plant, and animal world are used for treatment based on data taken from controlled studies in toxicology. The two guiding principles of homeopathy are the Law of Similars (like cures like) and the Law of the Infinitesimal Dose (the most potent remedies are those in the greatest dilution). The belief is that the remedies retain their effect because of electromagnetic frequency imprinting. The cardinal doctrine of homeopathy is that there is a vital force in the body that strives for health. Disease or disruption of this force cannot be classified but is unique to each person.

ACUPUNCTURE is based on a philosophy that a cycle of energy flowing through the body controls health. Pain and disease develop when there is a disturbance in that flow. Needles inserted at certain points in the body can remedy that imbalance or disturbance and affect a therapeutic response elsewhere in the body.

8. Manual Medicine

This philosophy believes that improving the structure and functioning of the human body will improve health and treat many diseases.

BODYWORK includes therapies such as massage, deep tissue manipulation, movement awareness, and energy balancing. Principles include alteration of muscle and tissue through pressure or deep friction, movement, education and self-awareness, breathing and emotional expression. Some of the popular types of bodywork are massage, Alexander Technique, Feldenkrais, Rolfing, Aston-Patterning, Hellerwork, Trager, and Bonnie Prudden Myotherapy.

CHIROPRACTIC is based on the theory that we have an innate intelligence flowing through the central nervous system to regulate bodily functions. There must be a balance between the central, peripheral, and autonomic nervous systems that are all intimately related to the spinal column. Subluxations between vertebrae can cause compression of the spinal cord's nerve roots, resulting in disease in various parts of the body. Chiropractic spinal adjustments focus on removing obstructions to the nervous system flow.

OSTEOPATHY centers on the musculoskeletal components of health and illness since that system uses most of the body's energy. It is based on the interrelationship of structure and function. Tension, restriction, or inefficiency in the musculoskeletal system can waste energy, leading to a variety of health problems. Osteopaths use mobilization, articulation, release methods, soft tissue techniques, muscle relaxation, and cranial sacral manipulation.

9. Mind/Body Medicine (Psychoneuroimmunology)

This philosophy is based on the belief that our psychological and emotional components influence our physical health. Stress, coping skills, personality traits, social connectedness, and self-esteem all correlate with both susceptibility and resistance to physical illness. Some of the approaches used are art and music therapy, bioenergetics, guided imagery (visualization), dance and movement therapy, dream work, focusing, Gestalt Therapy, hypnotherapy, journaling, Jungian analysis, neurolinguistic programming, postural integration, primal therapy, psychodrama, psychosynthesis, rational emotive therapy, reality therapy, rebirthing, Reichian analysis, and transactional analysis.

10. Naturopathic Medicine

This is a distinct system of healing. It is a philosophy, science, art, and practice that seeks to promote health through education and the rational use of natural agents. Its principles are based on the concept that the body is a self-healing organism. It centers on six basic principles: 1) the healing power of nature, 2) treat the cause, not the effect, 3) first, do no harm, 4) treat the whole person, 5) the physician is a teacher, 6) prevention is the best cure. Many different modalities are used including nutritional therapy, herbs, homeopathy, acupuncture, hydrotherapy, bodywork, counseling, and lifestyle modification.

11. Spiritual Medicine

This philosophy refers to the wholeness and unity of our personal existence and to the integration of the many dimensions that make up that wholeness. That includes the biological, physical, intellectual, and religious dimensions. It encompasses our feelings, relationships, attitudes, values, goals, ethical principles and behavior, religious beliefs, and all that makes us fully human. Spiritual healing is rooted in the belief that there is a supreme being or universal energy at work in the world. Health and illness can be influenced by our connection with that being or energy. This supreme being or energy is known by various names including God, Goddess, Allah, Krishna, Brahman, the Tao, the Universal Mind, the Almighty, the One, chi, prana, the Great Spirit, love, the Life Force, and the Absolute. Prayer, meditation, and alignment with divine energy are most important in spiritual medicine. Prayer may involve asking something for one's self or for others. It also may involve confession, lamentation, adoration, invocation, and thanksgiving. Prayer is nonlocal: infinite in time and space. Prayer is not sending energy, so the Divine factor in prayer is internal, not external. Therefore, in essence, all spiritual healing is a form of self-healing, since it is believed that the Divine is present in all individuals. Spiritual medicine can include a belief structure, a sense of meaning in one's life, a sense of connection and belonging, or religious views and traditions.

Appendix B
Complementary Treatments Used by Diane

Nutrients and Herbs

Cabbage juice. Every morning for six months, Bill prepared half a cup of freshly juiced cabbage mixed with half a cup of carrot juice to improve the flavor. Certain chemicals in cabbage are believed to support the body's estrogen detoxification and thereby counteract breast cancer.

Diet. Diane ate a balanced but not restrictive diet. She increased her intake of fruits and vegetables, especially the cruciferous family, like cabbage, broccoli, and cauliflower, which are abundant in antioxidants. Cruciferous foods also speed up estrogen metabolism and removal from the body, which may help to suppress breast cancer. Diane loved chocolate (which contains antioxidants) and other treats and continued to eat them with great pleasure.

Herbal Medicine. Diane visited Papa Henry Ausae, now deceased, a *kahuna la'au lapa'au* (expert herbalist healer) who lived in Hilo, Hawaii. She found his words comforting and used the herbs he suggested.

Marijuana. To counteract the nausea caused by chemotherapy, Diane occasionally brewed a tea with marijuana. She also tried Marinol, the pharmaceutical equivalent of marijuana, but that was only minimally effective.

Multiple vitamin/mineral tablets plus extra carotenoids. Diane took a daily multivitamin with carotenoids, a group of pigments in fruits and vegetables that include alpha carotene, beta carotene, lycopene, lutein and many other compounds that may have cancer-fighting properties.

Myers Cocktail. Bill mixed and administered an intravenous vitamin and mineral drip twice a week during Diane's chemotherapy to reduce side effects. Used to treat various illnesses, this cocktail also appears to strengthen the immune system. For more information about the Myers cocktail, see www.drlglass.com/myers.htm.

Shark liver oil. Studies have shown that squalamine, a substance found in high concentration in shark livers, suppresses the formation of new blood vessels in solid tumors, and may therefore be useful in halting tumor growth. Diane found that taking a shark liver oil capsule twice daily helped prevent fatigue during radiation treatment.

Soy. Diane increased her intake of soy, which contains a phytoestrogen, a plant-based estrogen-like chemical that may be antagonistic to breast cancer. Soy also is a source of protease inhibitors, which are anticancer and antiviral agents. There is controversy about the effects of soy on cancer, and some breast cancer survivors limit their intake to eight ounces of soy milk per day until more research is available.

Tea. Essiac tea contains burdock root and sheep sorrel herb, two herbs known to suppress cancer cells. Two other ingredients, slippery elm bark and watercress herb, are believed to strengthen the immune system and facilitate the removal of dead cancer cells. Some essiac teas contain other herbs such as Turkish rhubarb root, kelp, blessed thistle herb, and red clover blossom. Bill made a cup once or twice a day and served it to Diane either hot or cold.

Energy Work

Acupuncture. In acupuncture, thin needles are inserted at specific physical spots to stimulate certain organs and systems and release energy blockages. Diane received acupuncture treatments as needed to boost her immune system and to help relieve itching and nausea.

Healing Touch. Diane received regular Healing Touch treatments from her nursing friends. Healing Touch uses gentle touch and hand movements to balance energy, reduce stress, and support the immune system.

Holochromatic healing. Diane worked with Jamie Champion, creator of an integrated approach of healing modalities, including nutrition, herbs, detoxification, psychology, sound, and affirmations. Jamie Champion believed that during her years as a psychotherapist, Diane took on the pain and sorrow of clients with whom she worked, a common occupational hazard for therapists and other healers. He worked with Diane to clear old energy blockages and to eliminate physical and emotional toxins. For more information, consult www.mycolorprint.com.

Massage. Massage involves the manipulation of the body's soft tissue, which can increase circulation, promote relaxation, and help to detoxify. Diane received periodic massages from friends, family members, and professionals.

Meditation. Meditation is the practice of focusing one's mental energy. It often involves specific breathing techniques. Diane meditated daily to help calm her mind and body, and thereby promote general health.

Prayer. Diane prayed and gave gratitude daily as a means to connect with the Divine and to receive positive energy. Family members and friends prayed for her, individually or as part of prayer circles.

Qigong. Qigong, which means "energy cultivation," is an ancient Chinese healing art that focuses on breathing and movement to strengthen the mind-body connection. Diane practiced daily Qigong exercises at home and had healing sessions with Chunyi Lin in Minneapolis. For more information, consult www.learningstrategies.com/MasterLin.asp.

Reflexology. Reflexology is based on the acupuncture system, but involves deep massage of pressure points in the hands, feet, and other areas of concentrated energy. Its purpose is to release and balance any blocked energy. Diane received periodic reflexology treatments.

Emotional/Social Support

Camping. The Boundary Waters Canoe Area in northern Minnesota was one of Diane's favorite places. She and Bill continued to go there throughout her illness. They also car-camped in Minnesota parks, using a large tent given to them by their children. This tent allowed them to sleep on cots, which were more comfortable for Diane than sleeping on the ground.

Cancer group. When Diane was diagnosed with breast cancer, she organized a women's cancer support group at the Open Door Clinic in Mankato. Twelve women met monthly and shared their stories, information about treatments, and understanding of each other's challenges. The group, now called "Diane's Hope" in honor of its founder, is still meeting monthly.

Friends and family. Quality time with Bill, friends, and family helped Diane maintain a positive attitude. She allowed herself to be frightened or angry when those feelings arose, but her main focus was on enjoying every day with the people she loved.

Healing rituals. Many people close to Diane initiated and participated in healing rituals for her. One ritual included drumming in the woods with her closest friends. The amulets given to her by friends represented their good wishes and healing energy.

Letters and calls. People's greetings and wishes were a blessing to Diane. She would meditate on the cards and letters she received.

Spiritual activity. Although Diane did not ascribe to a particular religion during the last decades of her life, she maintained a deep spiritual life, read widely the works of spiritual teachers, recognized the healing power of rituals and prayer, and spent as much time as possible out of doors, connecting with the spiritual power of nature.

Walking. Diane loved the outdoors and tried to be outside for at least an hour most days. She logged two to four miles of walking several times a week, usually with a friend, and she treasured the time to nurture those relationships. Diane also organized a Cancer Walk along the Blue Earth River and through Sibley Park. Almost a hundred people participated in this educational event designed to raise awareness of common environmental causes of cancer.

Watching birds. Diane would watch the birds in the back yard, where a feeder and bird bath were set up. Their antics could amuse her for long stretches of time.

Attitude

Affirmations. Diane spoke and sang affirmations every day to strengthen her immune system and help maintain a positive outlook.

Carrying on with life. Diane loved her life and was determined to enjoy her students, colleagues, community, friends, and family. After the cancer returned, she continued to teach, attend board meetings, and travel. She even redecorated the living room, painting the walls her favorite shade of yellow.

Financial freedom. Diane found that giving herself permission to spend money on integrative healers, energy work, travel, family, friends, and pleasing gifts for herself and others helped foster a feeling of abundance and nurturance.

Flowers. Diane kept fresh flowers and plants in the house. Sometimes they were gifts; other times she bought or cut them herself. She believed, and research shows, that flowers and houseplants can improve the immune system.

Positive imaging. During her chemo treatments, Diane pictured the chemicals flowing into her as good and helpful, rather than poisonous. During her radiation treatments, she called up images of favorite places or "beamed" herself to loved ones. She visualized her body as healthy as possible.

Writing. Diane kept a journal during her cancer years. She also wrote poetry, which she had seldom done before, and shared her poems with others. She took a writing workshop for people with cancer. She corresponded with people via cards, letters, and e-mails until the week she died.

Appendix C
Resolve to Get Organized

by Vanda Manahan, Ph.D.

[Note: The following is a reprint of an "Ask Dr. Manahan" newspaper column by Diane's sister-in-law. It appeared in the Mankato Free Press on December 21, 2004.]

Q. My dear niece was called to her mother's home several weeks ago. My sister-in-law had a disabling stroke at age 66. My niece's efforts to take care of her mother were complicated by lack of information about her mother's affairs. She had to search through several purses, a cluttered desk, night stand, medicine cabinet, and a couple of coat pockets to find what she needed. I am only 63, but this served as a wake-up call for me. I don't want to leave my children in a similar predicament. How can I get organized for some unfortunate eventuality?

A. A useful New Year's resolution for any adult would be to gather and organize important information in a secure but accessible place. For seniors and the Baby Boomers fast approaching senior citizen status, this project is essential. The following tasks should be completed, the documents placed in labeled files, and stored where trusted family members are instructed to find them in the event of serious illness, disability, or death. Do not put these materials in a safe-deposit box because family members will need immediate access.

1. Prepare a durable power of attorney permitting a trusted family member to act legally on your behalf if you are unable to sign checks, enter into contracts, or sell property. You can specify and limit the powers you wish to grant.
2. Create or review your advance health care directive to guide a decision-maker if you become unable to speak for yourself. Be sure that your directive complies with the legal requirements of your state. If you have a sum-

mer or winter residence in another state, be sure that your directive complies with requirements in that state as well. As these documents are fairly general, attach a statement about your values should you have a terminal illness or major disability so that your health care agent will know your wishes.

3. Discuss your health care directive with the person you name to represent your wishes if you are unable to do so. Confirm that your representative is able to advocate for you. Provide a copy to your doctor, to the hospital, to family members, to any current care providers, and significant others. The information should lessen any future conflict.

4. Review and update your will. If an attorney holds the original, provide the name and address of the law office. Include a copy in your document file. If you are making informal bequests to family or friends, describe these objects and their designated recipients.

5. Gather important information such as copies of your Social Security number, your Medicare card, health insurance policies, prescription plans, and long term care policies. If you are a veteran or surviving spouse, include military records. It would be useful to make a master list of these identification numbers. One copy of the list could be kept in the file, another distributed to a child, and another kept handy in a purse or wallet.

6. Review financial information. Prepare a list of your assets, their value, and location. Include your bank accounts, pensions, stocks, annuities, certificates of deposit, promissory notes held on loans, as well as your debts, mortgages or monthly payments.

7. List the property that you own and the location of the deeds or abstracts of title and the titles to automobiles, boats, or other vehicles.

8. If you have a safe-deposit box, list the bank and the location of the key. Describe the contents in general terms.

9. If you have a pre-paid funeral plan, include that information.

10. Post the name and phone number of your primary physician by the phone, along with the other emergency numbers. Include the names, addresses, and telephone numbers of other health care providers such as dentist, ophthalmologist, or audiologist in your file.

11. Include copies of tax returns for the past five years.

12. List the names, addresses, and phone numbers of your bankers, accountant, financial advisor, and insurance agents.

13. Include an insurance file of life, homeowner's, renter's, automobile, disability, and/or accident policies.

Completing this project should give seniors and their family members a sense of accomplishment and security in knowing that information can easily be located when needed. The file should be updated at least annually.

Appendix D
An Open Letter to Tessa Manahan from Chuck Lofy

[Note: Chuck Lofy wrote the following letter to Diane's granddaughter, Tessa, on May, 17, 2001. He read his letter aloud at Diane's wake on July 16, 2001.]

Dear Tessa,

Yesterday, as you were leaving your grandparents' home to return to California, you were about to say goodbye to your Grandma Di when she asked you: "Tessa, what do you want to be when you grow up?" You looked up at her and said: "Grandma Di, when I grow up, I want to be a woman just like you."

Your reply made your Grandma Di very happy because it brought great joy to her to know that you love her so much that you want to be like her. It also made her sad because she would not live long enough to see you as the woman you want to become.

It is wonderful that you want to be like your Grandma Di. She is a very rare, bright, beautiful and special woman. She has so many remarkable qualities and talents that it may seem difficult to become like her. But not to worry. Grandma Di's greatest trait is that she is always, in everything she does, truly herself. What she wants for you, I am sure, is that you too will always be yourself. That will be the very best way to be like her.

I'd like to tell you some things about her so that, as you grow up, you will know what an extraordinary role model you have. Her life, and the person she is, can be a continual source of inspiration for you and for all of us.

More than anything else, your Grandma Di is a consummate friend. She is first of all a friend to the earth. She loves natural beauty and has always been at home in the northwoods, in the glory of Hawaii, on the shore of Lake Superior. She has traveled extensively in many parts of the world, always open to everything there is to see. She is always grounded in the earth, in her body, in her senses. I remember when she first began to do long distance running she told me how good it felt to be drenched with sweat and how much she even enjoyed the freedom of farting a time or two along the way.

Her groundedness in her physical world is basic to who she is. She sees in you that same at-homeness with your body, Tessa. Grandma Di appreciates and enjoys her body and all those things that give pleasure, such as eating, playing, and loving. She is not afraid of pleasure. In fact, she often teases about pleasure, about those things she enjoys—like M&Ms, a good massage, just gazing silently for a long time at the boundless waters of Lake Superior. One of the things I love most about Grandma Di is the playfulness she has about her body. Some of the best laughs she, Grandpa Bill, Mary (my wife) and I have had together were about normally unmentioned joys.

Grandma Di loves life. That is why it is so tragic to think of her life being cut short. Her illness is like a cruel joke that is almost impossible to accept. It makes me, all of us, want to scream out in pain, horror, shock, and disbelief. We all "rage against the dying of the light." But if there is anything she leaves for all of us, or anything that will make you like her, it is that great openness to life in all its color, sound, feel, and touch, and yes, even pain. Grandma Di is most alive in and through her senses. That is a distinguishing characteristic of hers. You'll enjoy being like her in this.

But if Grandma Di is a friend of the earth and of her body, she is also a friend to most of those she knows. To Grandpa Bill most of all! But also to your parents and her other children, and to you and her other grandchildren. And also to her countless women friends, including her "soul sisters." And to so many other friends too numerous to mention. And to me! Why is she such a friend? Because she listens to, and takes others in, as if each person she sees is the only one in the world at that moment. She attends to us! She focuses on us, listens to what we have to say, but looks deeper into what is going on beneath what we are saying. She always listens to who we are at that particular moment, at what is stirring deep within us. For this reason we all open up readily to her, tell her things about ourselves we didn't even know about ourselves, or things we thought we would keep private. She generates a sense of trust and safety in everyone she knows. That is one reason why she is such a good therapist, and teacher, and mother, grandmother, sister and wife. So, to be like her when you grow up, you will want to listen deeply, care deeply, to those you meet. Make everyone feel that when you are talking to them nothing else matters except what they have to say to you right then and there.

And then, to be like her, you will want to *learn* everything you can about others and about this world. Grandma Di is humble, always curious, and *always* learning. Even with her cancer she is always learning. She has two Master's degrees. She is always going to conferences, speeches, and seminars; forever going to concerts, plays, and movies. She loves to read and converse, and always wants to look at all sides of any issue. She is always looking for hidden pearls or gold nuggets, even in unlikely places and with unlikely people. Commit yourself to learn all you can, all your life long, Tessa. Grandma Di will love that.

Grandma Di has always been a creative and imaginative innovator. A good example of this is when she invited my daughter, Annmarie, who was then only twelve years old, to be a partner with her in facilitating a children's health group. Underneath this brilliant intuition was Grandma Di's great sensitivity to those she works with. She was able to get inside the children's world and understand how helpful it would be for them to have someone their own age, or just a little older, to relate to. Another place her creativity shows up regularly is in her teaching and speeches. Her approach is always personal and original. Everything she does comes from deep inside her. She is ahead of her times in many aspects of her life. She is always real, and always her own person. She has been a model for many, many women, as she will be for you.

You seem to have amazing athletic agility, Tessa. That is good. You will need that if you are to be like Grandma Di. She is a superb athlete. I told her once she is an incarnation of Diana, the goddess of athletes. I remember well the day she ran the marathon (26 miles!!) on a gorgeous autumn day in the Twin Cities. I ran fourteen miles with her before fading off. She was strong and magnificent that day. Grandma Di loves many sports: tennis, skiing, swimming, walking, you name it. She is an athlete in a family of athletes. You'll definitely want to live out that part of yourself to be like her.

You will also want to laugh a lot, to be like her. Grandma Di's whimsical humor has brightened many of our days. She is an imp who delights in stepping outside the usual, to see the unexpected, to step off the beaten path. She has an eye for fun and mischief. This is how she creates a sense of freshness about her. Her capacity for sheer delight is unmatched.

Perhaps you might find it difficult, Tessa, to be as honest, loyal, and immediate as is Grandma Di. It is impossible in Grandma Di's presence not to tell the truth. In fact, you do not *want* to lie when you are with her. She is so truthful herself that she simply calls out honesty in others. Yet she is always gentle with the truth. She never accuses or backs others in a corner. She "gentles" the truth out of others, without any trace of coercion.

Grandma Di's loyalty is beyond measure. She binds her friends to her heart with unbreakable bonds. She is indeed the very embodiment of friendship. She will be a standard of friendship for you as she is for all of us. So to be like her you will want actively to cultivate friendship. You will want to make friendship happen! You will not allow good friendships to die for lack of nourishment. Someone once wrote that a friend is "a masterpiece of nature." That is certainly true for Grandma Di. She is the Ultimate Friend.

I will tell you that Grandma Di is a very beautiful woman. Her blue eyes, her sparkle and smile, her warmth, her wit and sense of fun, her sensuality, her love of life all combine to make her a radiantly attractive woman. Yet her beauty always is natural, spontaneous, never forced or coaxed. She never seems particularly conscious of how beautiful she is. She loves nice clothes and surrounds her home with beautiful objects from all over the world. She loves flowers and all things bright and beautiful, like you!

Do you like to sing, Tessa? To be like Grandma Di you will want to sing a lot!! She has a beautiful voice. I used to love to sing with her as we washed dishes after a meal. One of the saddest things about cancer is that it affected her voice so much that she couldn't sing as much or as well as before. She also learned to play the cello, another example of her ceaseless desire to learn, grown and try new things. I think you already share with Grandma Di a great lust for life.

So there is a very good chance, Tessa, that you will in fact grow up to be a woman like Grandma Di. She will leave countless pictures, writings, and stories behind that will be there for you to read and study. Learn all you can about her. The more you learn about her, the more you will continue to be amazed at what an astonishing woman she is. You will be perfectly proud of her. You will love learning more and more about her. She will be your North Star, a beacon all your life long.

It is such a tragedy that her life is being cut short. One of her greatest regrets will be that she will not see you grow up to be a woman. She loves you beyond all measure. You are the darling of her heart, the sparkle in her eye. When it comes time for Grandma Di to leave us, she will leave a part of her behind in all of us. All of us will be a lot better because of her, a little more alive, a little more attuned to the beauty that surrounds us, a little more sensitive to the suffering in the world, especially our own suffering of missing her. Perhaps the best things we can do to console ourselves and bless her memory will be to sing. Who knows? Or will it be to play? Or to hug one another? Or to go run a mile? Or to call a friend? Or to walk in the quiet woods? Some people leave behind a box full of memories. Grandma Di will leave behind a trainload of memories, stories, pictures, and dreams. Oh, how blessed you are to have known her even for the shortest of times. May her spirit always guide and inspire you, Tessa. May you become a woman just like her!!

Chuck Lofy

Friend of Grandma Di

Granddaughter Tessa with Diane, 2001

Appendix E
Eulogy from Susie Symons

[Note: Susie Symons e-mailed a letter to Diane on May 13, 2001, after Diane's liver began to fail. Diane loved the letter so much that she asked Susie to read it at her Life Celebration. Here is the text of Susie's eulogy, a revised version of that letter.]

Darlin' Diane,

You have been "my woman"—my wisest, my steadiest, my most trusted friend for almost 30 years. You shared your wisdom, fairness, and humor, while always being an ally...absolutely on my side. For three decades, whenever we connected, I was replenished...like taking a long drink of pure, cool water after a walk in the desert.

You have been so influential in my life, Di-Girl—who I've become, how I choose to live, what I focus on (and also what I decide to let go of.) I can't count *all* the ways, but let me name a few.

For as long as I've known you, you've helped me to appreciate the majesty, mystery and subtlety of nature in deeper and honoring ways, creating a nest in which my spiritual self could later grow. In 1978, as we walked around Mountain Lake on Orcas Island in Washington, you stopped abruptly, awestruck by sunlight streaming through the huge cedars; that day *I* saw light in a new way too. I still think of you when I see sunlight coming through clouds. Being with you, I came to enjoy the gentle loveliness of Minnesota's cornfields in the fall, and the color of willow tree buds in the spring. For decades you've said, "I *crave* being outside!" In Hawaii in November 1999, you took very early morning walks while I slept. You told me, "Being outside is my meditation and my medicine and my healing."

Secondly, you've always been a model for justice and awareness. In the early 70s, you traveled from Oklahoma to walk in the Mother's March on Washington to protest the Vietnam War. Not only were you challenging the *status quo* nationally, you were revolutionary in your own kitchen too. In 1974, you negotiated with Bill for him to take over the duties of menu-planning, shopping, cooking, and cleaning up for one weekend each month. It was unheard of back then to ask that of a man, and it had a huge ripple effect in the homes of your friends, and that still continues. Moreover, this feminist agreement has been integrated by the next generation. Because our kids grew up seeing dads sharing in housework and meal-making, they've taught their spouses the equality you initiated. You were active, took steps, and were my best example of the phrase, "Think globally and act locally." Time and again I watched you create social justice in every community you were a part of.

There was one time in particular when John and I needed your thoughts on equality and social justice. It was when our son Johnny told us he was gay. We were surrounded by bias and lousy information, and I felt confused and "in the closet" myself. You said, "Susie, everything in current research tells us that loving someone of the same sex is just another way of being human. By the time our kids reach our age, homosexuality will be considered a genetic variable, like being left-handed or having freckles or green eyes. It may not be the dominant trait, but it's still normal." I felt such relief! There you were once again: hope-holder, truth-teller, teacher. You and Bill have challenged out-dated and formulaic thinking, whether in medicine, politics, or relationships. And yet you are the bearers of the *finest* traditions—in family, community, friendship, correspondence, wellness, and ritual.

Diane, you have given me, by being yourself, the greatest gift you could: for thirty years you have shown me how to be the adult woman that I want to be. And you have been *in love with life,* showing me how to be, every step of the way.

I have tried to find some meaning in your untimely death. For now, this is what I sense is true: yours is a wise and old soul. You've learned life's lessons in the eons that preceded this time. In *this* lifetime we have shared, it took you only six decades more to complete your work—to learn what *you* needed to learn, and then to teach and heal us.

Our spirits are there with you, Darling Diane. We are with you always, as you are always with us. As you continue on into the next state, whatever that may be, I know that you will come to me in ways that I cannot now imagine. I will always be ready to have you touch me, and continue teaching me, however you can. And I believe that when I die, your spirit will be waiting for me on the other side, ready to embrace me and comfort me, as you always have.

I love you, my Beloved Friend.

Susie

Appendix F
"Diane's Song"
by Jon Olseth

We take a walk in the late afternoon.
And we move through the trees and the bees—kicking leaves
and it always goes too soon.

And we talk about so many things while the sky makes its evening wings
to midnight blue.

And there's you shining through.

You hold my hand to see me through.
And you quietly smile with your eyes and buy me a cup or two.

And you understand how it goes and how nobody seems to know when
the pain comes due.

And there's you shining through.

When the stormclouds move through I see a dimple in the moon—
and that's you shining through.

Another heatwave in June—but the strawberries are ready soon.

Oh—July—the yards are full of the fireflies—
and that's you shining through—

I need you—Shining through.

[Note: Jon sang this song for Diane July 3, 2001, eleven days before her death. She loved it. He performed it again the day of her life celebration. The next summer, Jon recorded "Diane's Song." As he drove away from the recording session, he suddenly realized what day it was: July 3, 2002.]

Appendix G
Timeline of Diane Jansen Manahan

1940 Born in Faribault, Minnesota, to John and Merle Jansen on August 6; named Mary Diane.

1951 Met her future husband, Bill Manahan, in sixth grade of Madelia Elementary School, Madelia, Minnesota.

1958 Graduated from Madelia High School.

1962 Graduated from St. Olaf College, a Lutheran school in Northfield, Minnesota, with a B.S. in Nursing; began working at the Veteran's Administration Hospital in Minneapolis, Minnesota.

1964 Married Bill Manahan in St. Mary's Catholic Church in Madelia.

1965 Welcomed adopted baby Michael into her and Bill's home.

1967 Gave birth to David in Santa Barbara, California, where Bill was interning; volunteered as a nurse at an aboriginal hospital outside of Kuala Lumpur, Malaysia, where Bill began serving in the Peace Corps.

1968 Gave birth to Timothy in Kuala Lumpur.

1969 Volunteered at a girls' vocational school in Accra, Ghana, where Bill served in the Peace Corps.

1970 Gave birth to Christopher (Topher) in Arizona and returned to Africa twelve days later; served as a volunteer in a school counseling program in Oklahoma City where Bill completed his residency.

1973 Moved the family to Mankato, Minnesota where she started to work part time with the Mankato Psychiatric Clinic and Bill practiced family medicine; entered a Master's degree program.

1975 Father died of congestive heart failure.

1976 Earned a Master's Degree in Continuing Studies with a concentration in Counseling and Psychology; hired by the Mankato Psychiatric Clinic as their first female therapist.

1977 Mother died of non-smoker's lung cancer.

1978 Moved the family to Oahu, Hawaii, where Bill worked at a rural, underserved clinic; she took piano and hula lessons; and began to run seriously.

1981 Received certification as a clinical specialist in adult mental health/psychiatric nursing; joined the Mankato YMCA Board of Directors, serving through 1986.

1982 Finished the Twin Cities Marathon, averaging ten-minute miles.

1985 Joined the Wellness Center of Minnesota, founded by Bill and family friend Chuck Lofy, where she did individual and group therapy for three years while continuing her work at the Psychiatric Clinic.

1988 On the faculty of a community-oriented primary care program at Carney Hospital in Boston, where Bill had a Bush fellowship to work as a community-oriented primary care physician; recipient of Mankato YWCA Outstanding Woman of Achievement Award.

1990 Became a member of Sigma Theta Tau International Nursing Honors Society.

1991 Started teaching mental health nursing at Mankato State University (later Minnesota State University, Mankato) as an assistant professor.

1992 Did volunteer work for six months with Bill in Kenya through the Minnesota International Health Volunteers organization; joined the Board of Directors of the Archaeus Project in Minneapolis and Waimea, Hawaii.

1993 Had hip replacement surgery; began playing the cello.

1994 Began serving on the Board of Directors for the Minnesota International Health Volunteers organization.

1995 Rejoined the Board of Directors of the Mankato YMCA; diagnosed with breast cancer in December.

1996 Had lumpectomy, chemotherapy, and radiation; received Master of Science degree in Nursing; joined the Advisory Board of the Mind-Body Center, Washington, D.C.

1997 First grandchild, Tessa, born to David and his wife Jill, soon followed by Jansen, born to Tim and wife Kate; founded and facilitated the Women's Cancer Group at the Open Door Health Center, Mankato.

1998 Received certification as a Holistic Nurse.

1999 Metastasis of inoperable cancer; third grandchild, Teliz, born to David and Jill; hiked in Norway with Bill to celebrate their 35th wedding anniversary; earned a second Master's degree in Nursing.

2000 More metastases of cancer; fourth grandchild, Owen, born to Tim and Kate; achieved tenure and promotion to associate professor at Minnesota State University, Mankato; nominated by faculty for the Nurse Educator of the Year Award.

2001 Began palliative/comfort care; planned for her death and her Life Celebration; finished teaching spring semester; died July 14, on the birthday of her sister, Patt, and one day before the birthday of her granddaughter, Tessa.

~

2001 Received posthumously the Nurse Educator of the Year Award from the Minnesota Association of Colleges of Nursing, November 2.

2002 Diane's memorial in Mankato's Sibley Park dedicated on August 6; Diane's Room at Minnesota State University, Mankato, School of Nursing dedicated on November 22.

Appendix H
The Family Tree

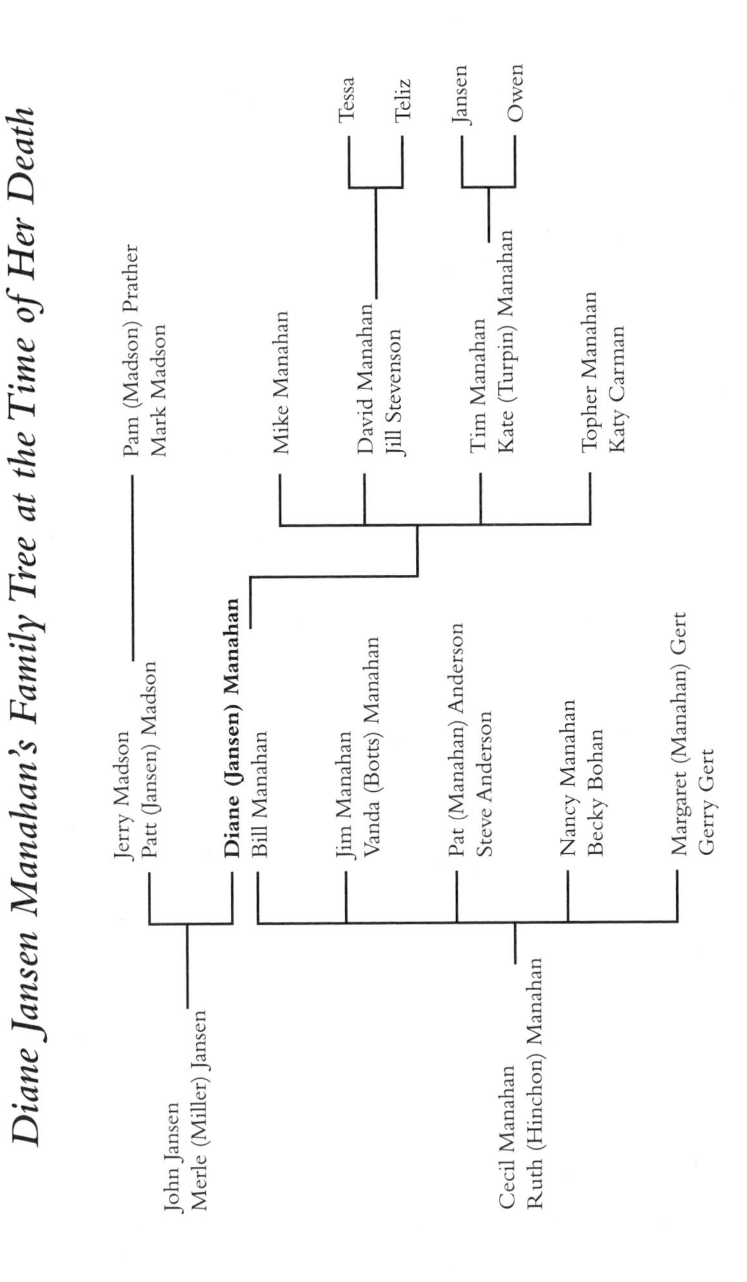

Appendix I
List of People Mentioned and Their Relation to Diane

Andy Lassen: Classmate from St. Olaf College. An architect and Los Angeles city commissioner.

Annmarie Rubin: Friend who co-hosted Diane's Life Celebration; daughter of Chuck and Mary Lofy; when twelve years old, joined Diane as a "co-therapist" in a children's group; a personal trainer, mother, and consultant.

Becky Bohan: Life-partner of Nancy Manahan, Bill's sister. A writer and business owner, now retired, living in Minneapolis.

Betsy Anderson Elias: Niece of Bill, daughter of Pat Anderson. A psychotherapist living in New Ulm, Minnesota.

Bev Palmquist: Close friend. Lives in Mankato, where she is in sales and marketing.

Bill Manahan: Husband of Diane. Father of Mike, David, Tim, and Topher. Physician and consultant in integrative medicine and Assistant Professor, Department of Family Medicine and Community Health, University of Minnesota Medical School; former president of American Holistic Medical Association; co-founder of Minnesota Wellness Center; author of *Eat for Health: Fast and Simple Ways of Eliminating Diseases Without Medical Assistance*.

Bob Christensen: Second cousin of Bill, a general surgeon in Minneapolis, now retired.

Chuck Lofy: Close friend. A semi-retired educational consultant living in Minneapolis with wife Mary; co-author of *Vitality: Igniting Your Organization's Spirit*.

Chunyi Lin: Diane's Qigong master practicing in Minneapolis.

Christiane Northrup: Former president of American Holistic Medical Association. Physician and author of *Woman's Bodies, Woman's Wisdom; The Wisdom of Menopause;* and *Mother-Daughter Wisdom: Understanding the Crucial Link Between Mothers, Daughters, and Health.*

David Manahan: Son of Diane and Bill, born 1967. Husband of Jill and father of Tessa and Teliz. Teaches Geography at the University of California in Davis.

Elizabeth Turk: Daughter of Laura and Jim Turk. Lives in Mankato where she works in Human Resources.

Hank Kolbinger: Mortician at Landkamer Johnson-Bowman Mortuary in Mankato, now deceased.

Jamie Champion: Nutritional consultant and energy healer. Developer of the ColorPrint Personality Profiling System.

Jansen William Manahan: Grandchild, son of Tim and Kate, born 1997.

Jill Stevenson: Daughter-in-law, wife of David, mother of Tessa and Teliz. A trained doula (pregnancy and birthing coach), intuitive, and energy worker.

Jim Manahan: Brother-in-law, brother of Bill and Nancy, and husband of Vanda. A semi-retired lawyer living in Mankato and consultant to Latin American countries in areas of legal reform and trial skills.

John Glick: Husband of Diane's friend Susie Symons. A professional potter living in Michigan.

John Lofy: Friend who co-hosted Diane's Life Celebration. Son of Chuck and Mary Lofy; a professional writer who lives in Ann Arbor, Michigan; co-author of *Vitality: Igniting Your Organization's Spirit*.

Jon Olseth: Husband of MaryPat Anderson, Bill's niece. An English teacher at Riverland Community College in Austin, Minnesota.

Kate Manahan: Daughter-in-law, wife of Tim, mother of Jansen and Owen. A community organizer and licensed Waldorf and public school teacher.

Katie Anderson: Niece of Bill, daughter of Pat Anderson. A psychotherapist living in Minneapolis.

Katy Carman: Daughter-in-law, now former wife of Topher. Lives in California.

Laura Turk: Close friend. Teacher and Mankato School District administrator, now retired.

Mark Madson: Nephew of Diane, son of Patt and Jerry Madson. Lives in Arizona, where he works for a utility company.

Mary Huntley: Friend and colleague at MSU,M School of Nursing, now retired; co-author of *A Mirthful Spirit: Embracing Laughter for Wellness.*

Mary Johnson: Friend and nursing instructor at St. Olaf College, now retired.

Mary Lofy: Close friend. An educational consultant who lives in Minneapolis with husband Chuck; co-author of *Vitality: Igniting Your Organization's Spirit.*

MaryPat Anderson: Niece of Bill, daughter of Pat Anderson, and wife of Jon Olseth. Physician who lives in Mankato.

Mike Manahan: Son of Diane and Bill, born in 1965. Lives in Mankato, where he works at a landscaping and nursery business.

MSU,M: Minnesota State University, Mankato, where Diane received her Master's degrees and taught in the School of Nursing; formerly called Mankato State University.

Nancy Manahan: Sister-in-law, sister of Bill. A writer and community college English teacher, now retired, who lives in Minneapolis with life-partner Becky Bohan.

Owen Turpin Manahan: Grandchild, son of Tim and Kate, born 2000.

Pam Prather: Niece of Diane, daughter of Patt and Jerry Madson. Lives in Arizona where she works in the insurance field.

Papa Henry: A *kahuna la'au lapa'au* (expert herbalist healer) who lived in Hilo, Hawaii, now deceased.

Pat Anderson: Sister-in-law, sister of Bill and Nancy. A clinical nurse specialist who lives in Madelia, MN and has an advanced nursing practice at the New Ulm Medical Center.

Patt Madson: Sister of Diane. A retired infection control nurse, who lives in Arizona with her husband Jerry.

Ruth Manahan: Mother-in-law, mother of Bill. Lived in Madelia until her death in 2003 at the age of 91.

Sister Ramona: A member of the School Sisters of Notre Dame located at Good Counsel Hill in Mankato. One of her many ministries was promoting women's friendships through support groups.

Sue Towey: Close friend. A private practice psychotherapist who teaches mind-body healing therapies at the University of Minnesota Center for Spirituality and Healing.

Susie Symons: Close friend. A private practice psychotherapist who lives in Michigan with husband John Glick.

Teliz Stevenson Manahan: Grandchild, son of David and Jill, born 1999.

Tessa Stevenson Manahan: Grandchild, daughter of David and Jill, born 1997.

Tim Kurlow: Mortician in Echo, Minnesota.

Tim Manahan: Son of Diane and Bill, born 1968. A Doctor of Osteopathy who lives in Maine with his wife Kate and two sons, Jansen and Owen.

Tom Giles: Son-in-law of Bev and Steve Palmquist. Violinist who played at Diane's Life Celebration.

Topher Manahan: Son of Diane and Bill, born 1970. A contractor/builder who lives in California with wife Ricki and their four children, Teddi, Jerri, Jordan, and Tommi.

Vanda Manahan: Wife of Jim Manahan, brother of Bill. Professor of Social Work at Minnesota State University, Mankato, now retired. Former contributor to the *Mankato Free Press*, where her column about the aging family ran weekly.

Recommended Resources

Internet Web site citations or sources may have changed since publication. Please let us know about any inaccuracies in any part of the book so that we may correct them in the next edition: info@nanbec.com

Alison's Gift: The Song of a Thousand Hearts Opening by Pat Hogan (NOSILA Publishing, 1999). The true story of seven-year-old Alison, rendered brain dead in a car accident. After she died in the hospital, her family cared for her body during a home vigil before she was cremated. The book, which inspired Diane to look at non-traditional ways of caring for her body, is available from www.crossings.net.

Bach for the Bath (Avalon Music, 2001). Adapted, orchestrated, and arranged by Michael Maxwell. www.avalonmusic.com.

Becoming Well Within Minnesota, a directory of integrative healing resources in Minnesota. www.becomingwell.org.

Beyond Knowing—Mysteries and Messages of Death and Life from a Forensic Pathologist by Janis Amatuzio (New World Library, 2006). A second book of inspiring experiences with families of those whose deaths Dr. Amatuzio has investigated.

Breast Cancer Action. A national organization working to transform breast cancer from a private medical crisis to a public health issue so that more research and funding go toward prevention and universal access to effective treatment. www.bcaction.org.

CaringBridge News. Provides a free website during a health crisis that can keep friends and extended family updated on diagnosis or treatment, and where messages for the patient can be posted. www.caringbridge.org.

Caring for the Dead: Your Final Act of Love by Lisa Carlson (Upper Access Publishers, 1997). A comprehensive guide to home deaths and funeral arrangements with state-by-state legal information compiled by the Funeral Consumer's Alliance. www.funerals.org.

Choices at the End of Life: Finding Out What Your Parents Want Before It's Too Late by Linda Norlander and Kerstin McSteen (Fairview Press, 2001). Two palliative care nurses offer guidelines for family discussions about advanced care planning, with useful examples and a glossary of hospice terms.

Coming to Rest: A Guide to Caring for Our Own Dead, an Alternative to the Commercial Funeral by Julie Wiskind and Richard Spiegel (Dovetail, Inc., 1998). A practical guide to a more comfortable, personalized after-death care of a loved one.

Conscious Living, Conscious Dying. A website on vital aging, conscious dying, and alternative death care, with links to Minnesota and national resources. www.lindabergh.org/links.htm.

Crossings: Caring for Our Own at Death. A resource center providing education and inspiration to families for better experiences in after-death care, with or without a funeral director, and for exercising choices that will bring about greater healing following the loss of a loved one. www.crossings.net.

Crossing the Threshold: Practical and Spiritual Guidance on Death and Dying by Philip Martyn and Nicholas Wijnberg (Temple Lodge Publishing, 2003). Based on Rudolf Steiner's teachings, this 69-page book includes practical and spiritual guidance on death and dying. It offers advice on the arrangement of funerals, laying out of the body, legal requirements and wills.

Death's Door: Modern Dying and the Ways We Grieve by Sandra M. Gilbert (Norton, 2006). Brilliant analysis of modern responses to death, combining literary commentary, cultural criticism, and reflections on the deaths of the author's baby and husband.

Dying at Home: A Family Guide for Caregiving by Andrea Sankar (Johns Hopkins University Press, 1991; second edition, 2000). An honest examination by a medical anthropologist of people's experiences caring for terminally ill family members at home.

The Final Act of Living: Reflections of a Longtime Hospice Nurse by Barbara Karnes, RN (BK Books, Inc., 2003). Signs of approaching death, living with a life-threatening illness, grief, living wills, and more. www.bkbooks.com.

Final Gifts: Understanding the Special Awareness, Needs and Communications of the Dying by Maggie Callanan and Patricia Kelly (Bantam, 1997). Longtime hospice nurses share intimate experiences with patients at the end of life. The "final gifts" are the peace and reassurance offered *to* the dying by their caregivers, and the comfort and enlightenment offered *by* the dying to those attending them.

Final Passages. Offers booklets of instructions for a home funeral and courses on personal and legal rights concerning family-directed funerals, cremation, and burial. www.finalpassages.org.

Five Wishes. A twelve-page living will for making plans in case one is incapacitated, seriously ill, or dying. www.agingwithdignity.org.

Forever Ours: Real Stories of Immortality and Living from a Forensic Pathologist by Janis Amatuzio (New World Library, 2004). A book of inspiring stories about end-of-life experiences by Minnesota's "Compassionate Coroner."

Funeral Consumers Alliance. A non-profit organization that provides information about affordable and meaningful funerals. www.funerals.org.

Gone from My Sight by Barbara Karnes, RN (BK Books, 2nd edition, 2005). A fifteen-page booklet concisely describing in layperson's terms the typical stages of the dying process during the weeks and hours leading up to death. www.bkbooks.com.

Grace and Grit: Spirituality and Healing in the Life and Death of Treya Killam Wilber by Ken Wilber (Shambhala; 2nd edition, 2001). Psychologist Ken Wilber's account of his wife's five-year ordeal with aggressive breast cancer. Killam, who died in 1989, combined orthodox treatment with therapies like diet, meditation, and psychotherapy. Wilber, while refuting the view that mind alone causes physical illness, presents cancer as "a healing crisis."

Graceful Exits: How Great Beings Die by Sushila Blackman (Weatherhill, 1997). Over 100 stories of how Buddhist monks have met death with grace and dignity.

Handbook for Creating a Home Funeral by Jerri Lyons and Janelle Va Melvin, 1998. Guidebook for dignified, legal, ecological, and economical alternatives to conventional funeral practices. www.finalpassages.org.

Health Journeys Resources for Mind, Body, and Spirit. Produces guided imagery audiotapes and CDs by psychotherapist Belleruth Naperstek and other healers. Some are specifically for use during chemotherapy. www.healthjourneys.com.

Hospice Care. A national organization offering valuable information and support for end-of-life and palliative care. www.nhpco.org.

Living into Dying: A Journal of Spiritual and Practical Deathcare for Family and Community by Nancy Jewel Poer (White Feather Publishing, 2002). Personal stories of caring for loved ones at the threshold of death and after, including vigils, building a casket, and practical aspects of caring for a body at home.

Living in Process: Basic Truths for Living the Path of the Soul by Anne Wilson Schaef (Wellspring/Ballantine, 1999). A model for living with authenticity and integrating the spiritual into all aspects of one's life. Includes inspiring real-life stories and wisdom from Native peoples around the globe.

A Mirthful Spirit: Embracing Laughter for Wellness by Mary Huntley and Edna Thayer (Beaver's Pond Press, 2007). A description of the benefits of humor for health, with tips for maintaining mirth for oneself, at home, on the job, and during times of stress.

The Needs of the Dying: A Guide for Bringing Hope, Comfort and Love to Life's Final Chapter by David Kessler (Harper, 1997). A classic guidebook for each phase of dying, endorsed by Elisabeth Kübler-Ross.

On Our Own Terms: Moyers on Dying. A four-part PBS documentary exploring more humane options for end-of-life experiences. 2006. http://www.pbs.org/wnet/onourownterms/index.html.

Pathways Health Crisis Resource Center. A Minneapolis center offering free classes and individual sessions for persons facing cancer and life-threatening or chronic illnesses. www.pathwaysminneapolis.org.

Pink Ribbon, Inc., by Samantha King (University of Minnesota Press, 2006). A critical analysis of the philanthropy, corporate stakes, marketing, and public policy that influence the perception and reality of breast cancer in America.

Rituals of Healing: Using Imagery for Health and Wellness by Jeanne Achterberg, Barbara Dossey, and Leslie Kolkmeier (Bantam, 1994). A practical guide for using the power of the mind and imagination to create rituals that help restore health.

Rudolf Steiner Press. Books by Rudolf Steiner and others on death, life after death, meditation, and spirituality. www.anthropress.org

Thin Places: Where Faith Is Affirmed and Hope Dwells by Mary Treacy O'Keefe (Beaver's Pond Press, 2005). An account of the death of Mary's parents and the "thin places" family and friends have experienced between the physical and spiritual realms. www.marytreacyokeefe.com.

University of Minnesota Center for Spirituality and Healing. Offers information on complementary and alternative therapies for common illnesses. www.takingchargecsh.umn.edu.

Well Within. A resource center in St. Paul, Minnesota, that assists people seeking balance and wellness while dealing with health challenges. Offers classes, support groups, Healing Touch, Qigong, massage, art therapy, counseling and more. www.wellwithin.org.

What Dying People Want: Practical Wisdom for the End of Life by David Kuhl (PublicAffairs, 2003). Helpful stories and suggestions for pain management, support groups, and initiating conversations about death, based on the physician-author's years of working with terminally ill patients.

Who Dies: An Investigation into Conscious Living and Conscious Dying by Steven Levine (Anchor, 1988). A death and grief counselor reflects on what it means to live life to the fullest. Includes recommendations for dealing with pain and preparing to die.

Bill on Diane's bench, Sibley Park, 2006

Acknowledgments

We are grateful to the many people who have been involved in this labor of love. Our deepest gratitude goes to Bill Manahan who answered our questions, read various drafts of the work, consulted on decisions about almost every aspect of the book, and was a continuing source of support. We also are indebted to Bill for giving us Diane's papers, which enabled us to share Diane's eloquent voice.

Special thanks go to Bill and Diane's sons and their wives who provided invaluable information, helped us piece together the sequence of events, and reviewed the manuscript: Mike, David, Jill, Topher, Ricki, Tim and Kate (who tracked down facts and sources and answered innumerable questions, and shared excerpts from her journal).

Thanks to others who allowed us to interview them and/or to include their words in this book: to Diane's sister Patt Madson, our first interviewee, who made us realize how moving the process of creating this book would be; Annmarie Lofy Rubin, Andy Lassen, Chuck and Mary Lofy, Jai Jeffery, John Lofy, Jon Olseth, Laura Turk, Mary Huntley, Pam Prather, Sue Towey, Susie Symons, and Tim Kurlow. To all the friends and family members we interviewed and who shared Diane stories that are not included in the book, we express our apologies and gratitude.

A special thanks to Robin Lewis for his design of the book cover and to Lynne Tuft for her support from her first listening to our experience of Diane's death to her advice on the cover design five years later.

Finally, thank you to the readers whose valuable feedback at different stages of the manuscript helped us to shape the book into its final form: Annmarie Rubin, Chuck Lofy, Deborah Woodworth, Jane Coleman, Jim and Vanda Manahan, Jon Olseth and MaryPat Anderson, Kelly Manahan, Laura Turk, Lynne Tuft, Mary Ellen Kinney, Mary Logue, Mary Treacy O'Keefe, Pat Anderson, Peg Cruikshank, Sandra Jo Palm, Susan Sobelson, Susie Symons, and Vicki Bohan. A special thank you to Ruth Baetz for her insightful manuscript analysis and rigorous editing. We appreciate the time and care that each of you devoted to Diane's book.

Permissions

Every effort was made to contact copyright holders to obtain permission to use the quotes in this book. If any work has been used without permission, we extend our apologies. Please contact us so that credit can be given in future editions of this book.

The following quotations fall within the realm of fair use: The excerpt from George Meredith's poem "Dirge in Woods" and the lines from Eleanor Farjeon's poem "Morning Has Broken" (set to music by Cat Stevens).

Thanks to Michael Mitchell for permission to quote from his song "Land of the Silver Birch."

Thanks to Vanda Manahan for permission to reprint her column "Resolve to Get Organized" from the *Mankato Free Press*, December 21, 2004.

Thanks to Diane Ackerman and to Random House for permission to use a stanza from "School Prayer" in *I Praise My Destroyer* by Diane Ackerman, copyright © 1998.

Flavia Weedn's poem "Some People" is reprinted with the permission of The Flavia Company.

The quote from Anne Lamott copyright © 1994 by Anne Lamott, is reprinted with the permission of the Wylie Agency, Inc.

"How to Help Someone during a Seizure" is adapted from *A*

Primer of Brain Tumors: Patient's Reference Manual, 8th Edition, 2004, p. 54. Used with permission of the American Brain Tumor Association.

The adaptation of Angeles Arrien's principles are from *The Four-fold Way: Walking the Paths of the Warrior, Teacher, Healer, and Visionary* (Harper Collins, 1993, pp. 7–8).

"Shalom to You," Elsie S. Eslinger, ©1983, The United Methodist Publishing House. (Administered by The Copyright Company c/o The Copyright Company, Nashville, TN.) All rights reserved. International copyright secured. Used by permission.

About the Authors

Nancy Manahan, Ph.D., is a community college English, women's studies, and film studies teacher, now retired. Her writing has appeared in numerous journals and anthologies. Her books include *Lesbian Nuns: Breaking Silence*, a groundbreaking anthology published in eight languages, and *On My Honor: Lesbians Reflect on Their Scouting Experience.*

Becky Bohan earned her M.A. in English Literature from the University of Wisconsin-Madison. She is the retired Vice-President of Knowledge Design and Delivery, Inc., a training consulting company. She has published a suspense novel, *Sinister Paradise*, and a mystery, *Fertile Betrayal.*

Nancy and Becky grew up in Madelia, Minnesota, Diane Manahan's hometown. Both received their undergraduate degrees in English from the University of Minnesota, Minneapolis. They make their home in Minneapolis.

Nancy and Becky are available to share their experiences of *Living Consciously, Dying Gracefully: A Journey with Cancer and Beyond* with groups. Please contact them for availability at info@nanbec.com.